A Handbook of Styles in
English Antique Furniture

A Handbook of Styles in English Antique Furniture

Brian Austen

W. Foulsham & Co Ltd

First published Great Britain 1974 by
W Foulsham & Co Ltd, Yeovil Road, Slough

© Brian Austen 1974

ISBN 0 572 00846 5

Photoset, printed and bound
in Great Britain by
REDWOOD BURN LIMITED
Trowbridge & Esher

Contents

Acknowledgements

The author would like to express his thanks to the following organisations and individuals:

The Department of Woodwork, Victoria and Albert Museum for facilities to undertake the sketching of pieces of furniture in their care and Mr G. C. Miller for undertaking the sketching and preparing of drawings for the work.

Mr J. Daniels of the Geffrye Museum for permission to photograph exhibits.

Messrs H. Blairman & Sons, M. Harris & Sons, Hotspur Ltd, Mallett & Son (Antiques) Ltd and Spink & Son Ltd for the loan of photographs.

Mr E. T. Joy for reading through the text and offering valuable advice throughout.

1 Seating Furniture

FEW CHAIRS made earlier than the sixteenth century survive. This is due not only to the long passage of time that separates the Middle Ages from our own day, but also because in the medieval period the chair was a symbol of status reserved for persons of consequence. Those of lesser position would be seated on benches or stools that must have been produced in considerable quantity. This aura of status given to chairs was less evident in the sixteenth century as they became a more common feature of house furnishing, but on formal occasions, and especially at court, it was well into the eighteenth century before it finally died out. When James I entertained the Constable of Castile at Whitehall in 1604 only the king and queen were provided with chairs and even the honoured guest sat on a stool provided with a cushion. A similar type of etiquette prevailed after the Restoration of Charles II, both at court and in private houses. Cosmo III, the Duke of Tuscany, when visiting Wilton House in 1669 permitted his host and hostess to be seated on chairs like himself as a special favour. The remainder of the company were provided with stools.

This no doubt accounts for the large number of stools listed in contemporary inventories. For instance, in 1590 Lord Lumley had in his various houses (Nonsuch Palace, Lumley Castle in Yorkshire, Tower Hill in London and Standsted in Sussex) 76 chairs, but also a total of 255 stools, 80 of which had some form of upholstery. It might also in part account for the practice that continued until the middle of the eighteenth century of including matching stools in suites of seating furniture, though in lesser numbers. In the sixteenth century the most common type of stool produced was probably that of trestle construction. These stools had boarded ends, seats and underframes and such shaping or carving as there was showed Gothic influence (plate 1a). Stools and benches of this type of construction were the work of carpenters. By the end of the sixteenth century, however, joined stools (known in contemporary inventories as 'joint stools') were becoming common (plate 1b). These were supported on four splayed baluster-turned legs, into which the frame and stretchers were mortised. As with all furniture of this period glue was not used to secure the joints, which were pierced to receive a dowel. Joined stools and benches required greater skill in execution and were the work of the joiner. Later stools follow similar stylistic trends to chairs, adopting upholstery in many cases from the beginning of the seventeenth century and after 1660 frequently having walnut frames (plate 17). Some examples of chairs and stools in walnut are known before *c.* 1660 and contemporary inventories point to many finer pieces of furniture of this wood, especially from the beginning of the seventeenth century. The survival rate of walnut furniture of this period is however low as the ordinary English Walnut (*juglans regia*) is liable to worm attack. Most of the furniture that remains is of oak, which was obviously the most commonly used furniture timber.

Chairs of a number of different types exist in the period from 1500 to 1660 and in most cases they incorporate frame and panel construction (figure 1). One of the earliest types, a survival from the Middle Ages, was of box construction with panels beneath the seat and arms. The example shown in plate 3 displays linenfold carving in the panels beneath the seat and in the back; this form of decoration was common in the fifteenth and early sixteenth centuries. The carved horizontal panel in the back with its crude imitation of Renaissance detail dates this chair to the second quarter of the sixteenth century. Such chairs were heavy and cumbersome and designed to be permanently sited in one location, such as the raised dais found at one end of the hall in most houses of the period.

During the first half of the sixteenth century chairs of lighter construction were introduced in which the panels were no longer provided beneath the arms and seat. One of the earliest of this type was the caquetoire (plate 4). This was probably of French origin, its name deriving from the verb *caqueter* (to chatter), hence the alternative English name, the 'conversation chair'. Typical features of this type of chair are the tall narrow back and the widely splayed arms, which follow the shaping of the seat.* By the middle of the sixteenth century all chairs appear to have lost the panelling beneath the arms and seat. Joined or 'joint' chairs made after this date adopted a roughly standard pattern with a raked back of

---

*Although the term caquetoire has been universally used by writers to describe this type of chair, Peter Thornton in an article in *The Connoisseur* (February 1974) argues convincingly that the term ought rightly to be applied to seventeenth century upholstered chairs of the back stool or "fathingale" type (see page 12).

1a   Stool of trestle construction, oak, first half of
sixteenth century. The two splayed uprights and
underframing display shaping in ogee form.
(Victoria & Albert Museum)

1b   *right* Joined stool, oak, first half of seventeenth
century, with typical splayed, turned legs and
stretchers near ground level. (Geffrye Museum)

2 *below*   Bench, oak, first half of the seventeenth
century with carved underframe and single stretcher
between the ends. (Geffrye Museum)

3 Joined chair of box construction, oak, second
quarter of the sixteenth century. (Victoria & Albert
Museum)

4 *right* Arm chair of the caquetoire type, oak,
second quarter of the sixteenth century. The chair is
of a type probably introduced from France and the
carving on the back shows strong Renaissance
feeling. (Victoria & Albert Museum)

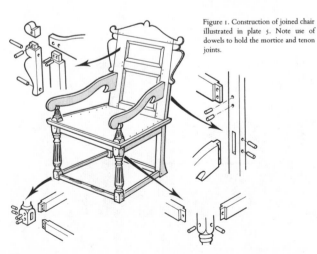

Figure 1. Construction of joined chair
illustrated in plate 5. Note use of
dowels to hold the mortice and tenon
joints.

frame and panel construction (plate 5). Backs were often carved and the
finer pieces displayed inlay and were surmounted by a carved cresting.
Stretchers were near to ground level and pegged as with the stools (figure
1). This type of joined chair retained its popularity until the Restoration,
but after *c*. 1660 was not made by the fashionable London trade, though in
country areas it survived for a further half-century. Such chairs are found,
in common with many items of furniture of this period, with dates carved
on them. Where the carving is in the form of bold raised numerals that
appear to be in keeping with the rest of the carving on the chair they can
probably be accepted as original, but dates shallowly carved into the
wood may be later additions. Settles of joined construction were made to
seat two or more people (plate 6) and both chairs and benches were made
on which the back was hinged so that it could be lowered onto the arms to
form a table if required (plate 7). These are correctly referred to as chair-
tables and bench-tables, though the term 'monks' benches' is in common
use in the antique trade. As most surviving examples date from roughly a
century after the dissolution of the monasteries this term would not appear
to be appropriate.

A further move towards portability in chairs occurred late in the sixteenth century, when lighter chairs without arms were produced. These
are known as back stools. By the beginning of the seventeenth century
chairs of this type were being upholstered and are generally referred to as
'farthingale' chairs (plate 8). Chairs made before this period for wealthy
patrons had sometimes been covered in fine imported cloths. The inventory of Henry VIII's furniture taken in 1547 shows that at Hampton Court
such chairs existed, though they may have been of foreign manufacture.
Other inventory references of this period are also known. Chairs and
stools were also made more comfortable by the use of loose cushions,
though fixed upholstery stuffed with wool or hair dates only from the
beginning of the seventeenth century. 'Farthingale chairs' were usually
covered in 'turkey work', a form of knotted woollen carpeting on a
canvas backing, often of floral pattern and inspired by the Persian and
Turkish rugs and carpets imported from Turkey (plate 8). For people of
consequence a more elegant upholstered armchair on X-frame supports
was developed at about the same date (plate 9). Such chairs derive from
prototypes dating back as far as the civilization of ancient Rome and the
X-frame support is also known from illustrations of medieval chairs. A
number of chairs of this type of early seventeenth century date survive at
Knole, Sevenoaks, Kent, where there is also a contemporary painting of
James I seated on such a chair.

The middle of the seventeenth century produced a number of distinc-

5 left Arm chair of joined construction, oak, with inlays in bog oak, cherry and various stained woods, first quarter of the seventeenth century. (Victoria & Albert Museum)

6 right Settle, oak, mid-seventeenth century, of frame and panel construction with turned legs and carving in top panels of the back. (Geffrye Museum)

7 below left Chair-table, oak, mid-seventeenth century, carved and with applied decoration. The chair back is hinged on pins and can be tipped over onto the arms to form a table. (Victoria & Albert Museum)

8 below Chair of the 'farthingale' type with seat and back covered with floral turkey work, oak, second quarter of the seventeenth century. (Victoria & Albert Museum)

tive types of chair. Yorkshire and Derbyshire chairs are examples of these. These usually have either two wide arched and carved crossrails forming the back members or two rails in the back connected by turned arcaded supports. In both types of chair the heavy panelled back of the joined chair is discarded (plate 10). Apart from the differences in the arrangement and decoration of the back rails both types display similar characteristics. In common with much oak furniture of the period they are decorated with applied split baluster work. Pieces of wood decoratively turned on a pole lathe were split down the centre and glued, in the case of these chairs, to the front of the uprights of the back. These uprights end in either an outward-facing or an inward-facing scroll. Legs are usually knob-turned. Yorkshire and Derbyshire chairs are believed, as the names suggest, to be distinctive North Country types of chair, though they bear similarities to chair types produced in Italy and Portugal. The carved mask of a man found on the crossrails of some Yorkshire and Derbyshire chairs is said to represent the head of Charles I and indicate the strong loyalty of many people in the North of England to the royalist cause.

Contemporary with the Yorkshire and Derbyshire chairs, but lacking the carving and decoration and therefore more in keeping with puritan taste, are the leather-covered back stools known as 'Cromwellian chairs' (plate 11), the leather being held in position with prominent brass-headed nails. All these types continued to be made after the Restoration of Charles II and some leather-covered chairs exist with carved front stretchers similar to those found on other types of chair that originated in the Restoration period.

The chairs so far described would have been mainly the work of the

9 Armchair of X-frame construction, beech, covered in velvet upholstery with matching footstool. Originally the property of William Juxon, Archbishop of Canterbury, who attended Charles I at his execution in 1649. (Victoria & Albert Museum)

10 *right* Chair, oak, of the Yorkshire and Derbyshire type, mid-seventeenth century. The shaping of the top of the uprights and the split baluster work applied to the front surface are common features of this type of chair. Seat panelled to accept a cushion. (Victoria & Albert Museum)

11 *below* Chairs, oak, of the 'Cromwellian' type with seat and back covered in leather. Twist-turned legs and front stretcher. Mid-seventeenth century. (Mallett)

joiner, with perhaps some turning of legs and stretchers sub-contracted to turners. Some chairs were, however, produced that appear to have been almost entirely the work of turners (plate 12). They are distinguished by their triangular seats and elaborately turned members for back, legs and stretchers. Existing examples appear to date from the late sixteenth and early seventeenth centuries but the design is of considerable antiquity and may probably be traced back by way of the Normans to Byzantine or Scandinavian prototypes.

Would-be collectors of furniture of this early period need to be warned that many pieces have been drastically altered, or have been made up in part from genuine material following the revival of interest in furniture of this period that took place in the nineteenth century after the publication in 1834 of Henry Shaw's book *Specimens of Ancient Furniture*.

With the restoration of the monarchy in 1660 a reaction set in against the puritan mood of the Commonwealth. Charles II had witnessed the higher continental standards of taste and craftsmanship during his exile in France and Holland, and the patronage of his court did much to raise standards of furniture craftsmanship in England. Foreign craftsmen of all kinds were attracted to England, in part by the ready patronage of the landowning and mercantile classes, and also in the case of French Huguenots to avoid the feared persecution by their Catholic neighbours, especially after the revocation of the Edict of Nantes in 1685. This had previously afforded them a degree of protection and independence.

In addition to this improvement in craftsmanship, new materials were adopted. Walnut now became the usual timber for fashionable furniture, and the use of oak and beech in the period following 1660 is often a sign of country craftsmanship. Walnut was to remain popular until about 1740, but its replacement by mahogany was assisted by a shortage of walnut that made itself felt from the first decade of the eighteenth century. Much walnut was imported, and severe frosts in central Europe in 1709 resulted in the destruction of trees on a considerable scale. France, one of Britain's principal suppliers, forbade further export from 1720. To some extent this gap in supplies was filled by the importation of Virginian walnut from the American colonies, which was favoured by the removal in 1721 of the duty on timber coming to Britain from the American colonies. This concession also favoured the importation of mahogany. Soon after the Restoration cane came into use as a material for the seats and backs of chairs and day beds (an early form of couch). This was imported from the Malay Peninsula as an article of trade by the East India Company and was in popular use up to c. 1730 (plates 13, 14, 15, 19).

12 Arm chair of turned construction, oak and ash, early seventeenth century. (Victoria & Albert Museum)

13 *above* Arm chair, walnut, with cane seat and back panel, *c.*1680. The elaborate carving and twist-turned back supports are typical of this period. The carved cresting, consisting of two cherubs holding a crown, is repeated on the carved stretcher beneath the seat. (Victoria & Albert Museum)

14 *left* Chairs, walnut with cane seat and back, *c.*1685. The very tall backs of chairs of this period and the matching carved cresting and front stretcher are characteristic. (Spink)

Chairs of the immediate post-Restoration period have light walnut frames of knob, bobbin or twist turning and are often described in contemporary references as 'turned all over'. From *c.* 1670 to 1700 most chairs have tall raked backs, perhaps matching the hairstyles of the ladies of the late Stuart court (plates 14 and 16). This was the period of Grinling Gibbons, the doyen of English wood carvers, who was himself reflecting the prevailing Baroque taste of the age. Thus the frames of chairs of this period are often elaborately carved and the broad stretchers at the front are arched and repeat the carved decoration of the chair top rail. Cherubs holding a crown between them are a common Restoration design, as is the carving of oak leaves. Walnut was a wood well suited to carving. Back supports are found decorated with twist turning while arms and legs end in the form of scrolls. Elaborately carved chairs of this type originated in France but the idea spread quickly to Holland and from these countries they were introduced into England. Upholstered chairs of this period often have less elaborate frames but are similar in general dimensions (plate 16).

From about 1700 a dramatic change in form occurred that was to produce the popular curvilinear chair known as the 'Queen Anne' type. The back was reduced slightly in height and the top took on a rounded outline. A single vertical splat of curvilinear form, both in plan and elevation, occupied the centre of the back, providing a considerable degree of comfort for the sitter. The cabriole leg terminating in pad or hoof feet was introduced, at first with stretchers (plates 18 and 19), though these were soon dispensed with as unnecessary. This basic shape was to be retained until the

15 *right* Day bed, walnut with cane seat and carved back and underframe stretcher, *c.*1685. The back-rest is adjustable. (Victoria & Albert Museum)

16 *above* Chairs, walnut, *c.* 1695, with upholstered
seat and back. Characteristic features are the tall
shaped backs not extending down to the seat frame,
the sinuous stretcher in X form with a finial at the
crossing, and the carved 'mushroom' caps at the top
of the front legs. (Mallett)

17 *below* Stool, walnut with turned legs and
stretchers and upholstered seat, *c.*1690. (Mallett)

18 *right* Chair, walnut with marquetry decoration,
*c.*1710. This chair shows an early form of the cabriole
leg ending in a simplified hoof foot, and incorporates
curved stretchers. Strong Dutch influence in the
design. (Victoria & Albert Museum)

end of the walnut period (*c*. 1740), but after the Hanoverian succession chairs became heavier in form and often more elaborate in detail. Carving in the form of shell, acanthus leaf, cabochon or satyr-head motifs appeared on the knees of the cabriole legs, which now often terminated in ball and claw feet (plates 20, 22, 23 and 26). The front seat frame was sometimes provided with an apron, which allowed further room for carving, often in the form of a shell. Better-class chairs of this period are often veneered in figured walnut. The carved decoration tends to become more pronounced after about 1720 under the prevailing taste of the architect William Kent, who was noted for his Baroque furniture designs and interiors. Settees to match sets of chairs may be found similar in form, consisting of two or more chair backs joined and standing on six or more legs. Arms of chairs and settees often terminated in lion or eagle heads (plate 20). Upholstered chairs with short cabriole legs sometimes have wings to the back (plate 25) and were in some cases originally covered in embroidery in petit-point (tent stitch).

During the Georgian period a number of specialized types of chair developed, one of the earliest being the library or reading chair (plate 21), which is known from *c*. 1720. These chairs were made with walnut, and after *c*. 1740 mahogany, frames. The seat, arms and 'back' were usually covered with leather and the reader would sit astride the seat facing the book rest. A drawer was provided under the seat for writing materials. These chairs are frequently referred to as 'cock-fighting' chairs but there is no evidence that they were designed for this purpose and Thomas Sheraton in *The Cabinet Dictionary* (1803) clearly states that they were 'intended to make the exercise of reading easy'. Roughly contemporary in date are the 'writing chairs' shown in plate 23, a type distinctive of the early Georgian period and often characterized by three legs at the front of the chair and two splats in the back. Although the term 'writing chair' has become attached to chairs of this type there is no evidence as to their precise function. A much longer-lived type was the hall chair, which was developed from the early eighteenth century and designed to stand in the entrance hall or corridors of large country or town houses (plate 24). The entrance hall, according to Robert Adam, was 'a room of access where servants in livery attend'. It was designed to impress the visitor with the taste of the owner of the house. These chairs were considered part of the decorative scheme and had much carved and painted decoration lavished upon them. The heraldic device of the family was often incorporated in the back. As servants were the only people likely to use them seats were not upholstered and the backs were solid and upright. Chairs of this type

19 *above* Chairs with carved and japanned frame,
c.1715. Note late use of cane in the chair back,
cabriole legs with carving on the knee and shaped
stretchers with a central finial. (Mallett)

20 *below* Armchair, veneered with burr walnut,
c.1720. The arms terminate in eagle heads while the
cabriole legs with carved shells on the knees end in
ball and claw feet. (Mallett)

21 *below* Reading chair, walnut frame, seat covered
in leather, c.1725. (Mallett)

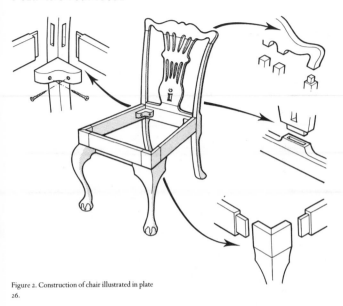

Figure 2. Construction of chair illustrated in plate 26.

were still in production in the middle years of Queen Victoria's reign. Long stools with scrolled ends were often used in halls in the late eighteenth century, while wooden hall benches are included in Victorian design books.

A popular country style of chair first appearing at the beginning of the eighteenth century was the Windsor chair (plate 34). It is first mentioned in 1724, when a chair of this type was used by Lady Percival at Hall Barn in Buckinghamshire. Most of the frame of Windsor chairs is usually of beech, ash or yew and an important centre for their production was the neighbourhood of High Wycombe in Buckinghamshire, where the beech woods of the Chilterns provided an ample supply of timber for the purpose. Elm was the usual wood for the solid seat. Chairs of this type appear to have been popular in inns and cottages and as garden chairs, though instances are known of their use in the library of Cannons, the house of the Duke of Chandos, in 1725 and in the Bodleian Library in Oxford in 1766. Although made to a traditional country design they did in some cases adopt certain features of the fashionable furniture of the

21

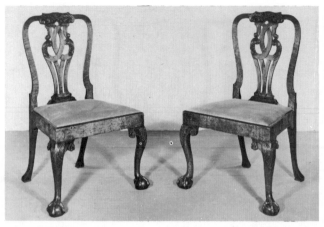

22 *above* Chairs, walnut, *c.* 1735, with drop-in upholstered seat and cabriole legs with carved acanthus leaf on the knee, and ball and claw feet. The splat in the back is pierced and carved and beginning to adopt certain characteristics pointing to the mid-century 'Chippendale' style. (Mallett)

24 Hall chair, mahogany, late eighteenth century. These chairs were used either in entrance halls or summer houses and were produced for appearance rather than comfort. (Hotspur)

23 *below* Writing chair, walnut, *c.*1740, with veneered seat frame, cabriole legs with acanthus carving on the knee and ball and claw feet. This type of chair is unique to the early Georgian period, and although called a writing chair there is no conclusive evidence that they were intended for this purpose. (Hotspur)

period in which they were made. Some Windsor chairs of the mid-eighteenth century, for instance, adopt cabriole legs and piercing in the Gothic style in the back.

By 1740 mahogany had taken over from walnut as the fashionable wood for furniture. At first a dense mahogany with little figure was imported, mainly from the Spanish West Indian island of San Domingo. This was being challenged by *c.* 1760 and was soon afterwards replaced by Cuban mahogany; by the end of the eighteenth century additional supplies were being brought in from the coast of British Honduras (baywood). Cuban wood showed attractive figure and markings and was largely used for veneering. Until the first decade of the twentieth century mahogany was to remain the most common wood used by fashionable furniture-makers for chair construction because of its great strength.

At first the changeover from walnut to mahogany had little effect on chair design, but by *c.* 1750 a style had developed that we associate with the name of Chippendale. Thomas Chippendale was the first man in Britain to issue a design book entirely devoted to furniture and his publication *The Gentleman and Cabinet-Maker's Director* (first edition 1754, second edition 1755, third edition 1762) shows designs for chair backs with shaped top rails and elaborately carved and pierced splats that are universally associated with his name (plates 28 and 29). Many of his published designs for chairs show delicate scroll feet, but in practice quality chairs of this period often still retain the ball and claw foot. The use of C and S scroll work in the back is a reflection of the Rococo taste that had been brought into England from France in the period following 1740.

Another design associated with Chippendale's name is the ladder-back chair, though this type is a traditional English design that antedates Chippendale's time and is not illustrated in the *Director* (plate 32). The 'Chippendale' chair proved very popular and was widely produced by many makers from about 1750 onwards. Even in country areas simplified versions of the design were produced in oak, beech and other native timbers, with straight, square-section legs.

Chippendale and other contemporary designers also produced designs for chairs in the Chinese taste, which was at the zenith of its popularity in the 1750s. Bedrooms especially selected for decoration in this style would have oriental wallpapers as well as furniture in the 'Chinese' taste. In most cases chairs in this form have straight legs with pierced brackets between the legs and the seat frame. The back is filled with geometrical fret patterns (plate 30). Blind fret-carving of a similar nature can be found on the seat frame and legs of chairs in this style (plate 27). The other fashionable

23

25 above Wing armchair, walnut, *c.*1720, on short cabriole legs, with shell motifs carved on the knees and club feet. This type of upholstered chair is very characteristic of the early Georgian period. (Mallett)

27 below Armchairs, mahogany, *c.* 1755. The legs and arms are carved with a blind fret pattern in the Chinese taste, and the brackets connecting the seat and the chair frame consist of two Rococo C scrolls. (Mallett)

26 above Chair, mahogany, *c.*1750, with drop-in seat covered with tent-stitch embroidery. The serpentine shape of the top rail (cupid's bow) and the introduction of C scrolls in the carving on the knee of the legs are signs of Rococo influence coming in from France at this period. (Victoria & Albert Museum)

28 *left* Chair, mahogany, *c*.1760, with shaped and pierced splat in the style of Thomas Chippendale. The legs are square-section with stretchers, though Chippendale's designs feature the cabriole leg for such chairs. (Blairman)

29 *below* Plate 16 of the 1762 edition of Thomas Chippendale's, *The Gentleman and Cabinet-Maker's Director* showing typical chair backs of the period. In practice chair-makers produced many variants. The chair in plate 27 has a marked resemblance to the third design

30 *bottom* Arm chairs, mahogany, *c*. 1760, in the Chinese taste with back and sides filled with geometrical fret, plain square-section legs and stretchers. (Mallett)

31 *bottom right* Chairs, mahogany, *c*. 1760, in Gothick taste. This shows particularly in the two quatrefoil piercings in the middle of the chair back. (Mallett)

style was the 'gothick' (plate 31) that was being 'revived' by enthusiasts such as Horace Walpole. In chairs of this type square-section legs and brackets between the seat frame and legs are also found, but the back design incorporates tracery inspired by that found in Gothic architecture. Upholstered chairs, often with gilt frames, show in many cases a resemblance to similar French pieces of this period with which Chippendale was clearly familiar as he had visited France and was an importer of French chair frames (plate 33).

The Rococo taste was to wane soon after 1760 when the architect Robert Adam was developing his distinctive form of neo-classicism. In addition to buildings and interior decoration Adam was very concerned with the furnishings of the rooms which he designed. As a result he often produced drawings for a range of furniture intended for the main reception and state rooms of the houses in which he undertook commissions. These included designs for chairs and settees. His chair designs incorporate motifs adapted from classical architecture and decoration, such as the lyre used in chair backs at Osterley Park in Middlesex and Nostell Priory in Yorkshire. Legs of the Adam period are usually straight, tapered and may end in spade feet, while the sinuous outlines of the Rococo are rejected in favour of straight or simple, curved outlines. The neo-classical taste introduced by Robert Adam for a few rich patrons was soon popularized and this phase is reflected in the designs of George Hepplewhite. His name is particularly associated with shield-back and wheel-back chairs (plate 35 and 36) though he was the originator of neither. His chair designs are decorated with strings of husks or bell flowers, paterae, urns and classical drapes from the Adam repertoire and some chairs incorporate the three feathers of the Prince of Wales.

Thomas Sheraton, a near-contemporary of Hepplewhite, is remembered for his chair designs with rectangular backs showing neo-classical influence (plate 39), though some of Hepplewhite's designs in the 1794 edition of the *Cabinet-Maker and Upholsterer's Guide* are in this form and Sheraton produced designs for shield-back chairs. It should be noted that in the case of neither Hepplewhite nor Sheraton is there any authenticated piece of furniture in existence, and the evidence suggests that both were designers of furniture rather than producers, though both were trained craftsmen. Painted chairs of beech, and satinwood chairs with painted designs (often of a floral character) date from this period (plates 36, 39 and 41).

Some Regency chairs from *c.* 1800 onwards took the love of classicism a stage further by trying to copy the forms of classical furniture as depicted on such objects as Greek painted vases. The Greek *klismos*, a chair featuring sabre legs and a pronounced shoulder board extending beyond the uprights of the back, was copied and was to have a pronounced influence on chair design in this period (plates 42 and 43). In other chairs the front legs took on the form of animal monopodia (plates 42 and 44), again following classical precedent. Another feature of Regency chair design was the use of a twisted rope motif in the backs of chairs, usually for the top or middle rail (plate 46). This is often incorporated in a distinctive type of chair of lighter construction on sabre legs and with an outward curving back introduced c. 1805 and referred to as a 'Trafalgar chair', in honour of Nelson's naval victory. Rosewood is found in use for chairs in the Regency period and its popularity for this purpose was to extend into Victorian times. Marquetry, which had been popular in the Adam and Hepplewhite designs up to c. 1790, was now out of fashion, but brass inlay was used on chairs as well as other pieces of furniture. It contrasted well with the dark lustrous woods then in use.

The reign of Queen Victoria (1837–1901) displays a multitude of differing styles, for designers not only delved into past periods of English furniture but sought inspiration in the past and present styles of other nations. Thus in 1833 John Loudon, the author of the *Encyclopaedia of Cottage, Farm and Villa Architecture*, could distinguish the Grecian, Gothic, Elizabethan and Louis XIV styles. The greatest original contribution to English chair design in the Victorian period was, however, the balloon-back chair, which in walnut and on cabriole legs has a grace missing

32 *above* Chair and arm chair mahogany, *c.* 1770, in ladder-back form, the horizontal rails and the top of the frame being sinuous in outline in the Rococo taste. (Mallett)

34 *below* Windsor chair, yew with elm seat, *c.* 1770. This chair, although of an established country type not produced in the fashionable town trade, nevertheless shows certain features associated with the popular chair styles of the period, e.g. cabriole legs ending in pad feet, the shaping of the arms and the piercing of the splat. (Mallett)

33 *below* Arm chair, mahogany, *c.*1770, showing strong French influence in the shaping of the arms, legs and seat frame. Legs are of cabriole form terminating in French scroll feet. (Blairman)

35 *right* Arm chair, mahogany, with upholstered shield-shape back. The front of the seat frame is carved with two flanking paterae and the round fluted legs are necked, *c.*1780. (Blairman)-

36 *below* Arm chairs, painted beech. The wheel-backs display an urn, drapes and foliage in the Hepplewhite style. Floral designs are painted on the chair frame, *c.*1785. (Mallett)

37 *left* Chair, elm and beech stained to resemble mahogany, *c.*1790. This is a country version of the fashionable Hepplewhite style and these simplified adaptions of the prevailing fashionable styles were produced in considerable numbers. (Private collection)

38 *below* Settee, gilt and carved, *c.*1780, in the style of George Hepplewhite and showing strong French influence. Straight fluted legs in the neo-classical taste of the time. (Mallett)

39 *above* Chairs, satinwood with painted decoration, *c.*1790. The painting takes the form of an urn on the top rail, classical drapes, and strings of bell flowers on the legs and the uprights of the back. Legs taper to end in spade feet. (Mallett)

40 *below* Chair, mahogany, *c.*1805, with round-section turned legs and wide top rail representing a transition from Sheraton to Regency characteristics. (Blairman)

41 *below* Chair, beechwood, japanned in black, *c.*1800. Seat rail decorated with Greek key pattern freize and seat caned. Oval cane panel in the back in the form of a patera with a painted panel in the centre. (Geffrye Museum)

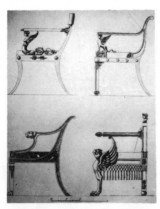

42 above Plate 55 of George Smith's *A Collection of Designs for Household Furniture and Interior Decoration* (1808). All the designs show considerable use of motifs taken from classical antiquity which is characteristic of much of the more elaborate furniture produced in this period. The first designs with its sabre legs is clearly inspired by the shape of the Greek *klismos*, a chair illustrated on Greek classical vase painting. A considerable influence in the spread of the taste for such furniture was Thomas Hope (see section on designers p. 142).

43 above Chair, mahogany, *c.*1810, showing sabre legs and high shoulder board in the back, both characteristics of Regency chairs. (Blairman)

44 below Arm chairs, gilt and carved wood with each front leg in the form of a lion monopodium terminating in a paw foot. This fashion based on classical precedent was fostered by the designs of Thomas Hope and George Smith. (Mallett)

45 *above* Arm chair, japanned in black and gold in
the Chinese taste, *c.*1810. The renewal of the Chinese
taste in the Regency was stimulated by the use of this
style in the interior decoration of the Royal Pavilion
at Brighton by the Prince Regent. The supports of
the arms are in the form of dolphins, another device
which enjoyed some popularity from *c.*1805.
(Blairman)

46 *above right* Arm chair, *c.*1810, of the type often
referred to as 'Trafalgar chair', with a twisted rope
device incorporated in the top rail. The panel in the
back is decorated with two anthemions (stylized
Greek honeysuckle motif). The shaping of the arms
ending in an open scroll is very characteristic of
Regency arm chairs. (Mallett)

47 *right* Arm chair in stained beech, *c.*1820. A
country-made chair with turned legs fashionable in
the early Regency period and high shoulder board of
rather narrow proportion. (Private collection)

48 *above* Chairs, painted, in Gothic taste, early nineteenth century. The increasing popularity of Gothic architecture in this period, not only for churches, but also larger domestic buildings, resulted in an increase in the amount of furniture produced in this style. It was still however a minority taste. (Mallett)

49 *below* Chair, beech gilt painted and carved, *c*.1834. It was designed by the architect Philip Hardwick for the Goldsmiths' Hall and was made by W. & C. Wilkinson. The cabriole legs with their scroll feet reveal a revival of French influence, while the cresting board characteristic of Regency chairs has adopted a curvilinear form. (Victoria & Albert Museum)

50 *below* Chair, mahogany, *c*.1850, with shaped seat frame, cabriole legs and buckle shaped back. Chairs with shaped seats were usually designed for drawing rooms while those with straight legs and seat frames were described as dining room chairs. (Private collection)

from much Victorian furniture. The design developed from the high shoulder board on Regency chairs, which by the 1820s was appearing with shaped ends and curved form. From this developed a chair with an oval back on either straight or cabriole legs (plate 50). These are usually in mahogany. Contemporary with these chair types is the button-back upholstered chair with its curvilinear form. Some Victorian furniture is bulky and hence unpopular, but chairs of this kind are well suited to modern homes and are in constant demand today (plate 51). Chairs in Victorian version of the 'Elizabethan' form are really copies and adaptions of high-back Restoration chairs and their tall, rigid backs make them uncomfortable, though when upholstered in their original Berlin wool work they are an attractive feature (plate 52). Another chair with a tall, rigid back of not dissimilar design was the *prie dieu* (plate 53). Upholstered chairs with gilt frames imitating the styles of the Louis XV French Rococo period and thus resembling certain designs of Chippendale were also extensively produced. Gothic chairs, usually in oak, were less common and confined mainly to the library. In most cases it was their carved decoration rather than their structural form that was suggestive of Gothicism and in this sense they were a continuation of the revived Gothic taste that originated in the mid-eighteenth century and enjoyed some popularity in the Regency period (plate 48).

A material new to chair construction in the early Victorian period was *papier mâché*. This was either pressed into shape or built up layer by layer in moulds. The finished chair was then japanned in black, inlaid with mother of pearl and painted, usually with floral designs (plate 54). The centre of the industry was Birmingham and the firm of Jennens and Bettridge were the leaders in this field. Their impressed stamp can quite often be found on pieces of furniture of this material.

The greatest influence in late Victorian design was the work of William Morris and his disciples. Morris saw the evils brought to Victorian society by the machine age; he saw craftsmanship threatened and was dedicated to its preservation. Morris was not a designer of furniture himself but the firm that he founded in 1861 (Morris, Marshall, Faulkner and Company) made and marketed ranges of furniture suited both to the rich patron and to those of lesser means. One of the company's most successful designs was the Sussex chair, based upon country types of chair still in local production at that time (plate 55). The ideas of simple, honest design and craftsmanship that Morris put forward encouraged other enterprises (known collectively as the 'Arts and Crafts Movement') based upon stimulating a pride in craftsmanship by allowing a workman to carry out

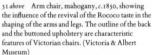

51 *above* Arm chair, mahogany, c.1850, showing the influence of the revival of the Rococo taste in the shaping of the arms and legs. The outline of the back and the buttoned upholstery are characteristic features of Victorian chairs. (Victoria & Albert Museum)

52 *above right* Chair, mahogany, c.1845, in the 'Elizabethan' taste. The twist-turned supports and legs and high narrow back are, however, much more characteristic of the Restoration period, c.1680. Upholstered with contemporary floral embroidered material (Berlin wool work). (Victoria & Albert Museum)

53 *right* Chair, walnut, c. 1850, of the prie dieu type, sometimes called 'devotional chairs'. The T-shaped back is typical of this type of chair as is also the contemporary floral embroidered upholstery material (Geffrye Museum)

54 *above* Chair, papier mâché, japanned, painted and gilded, *c.*1860. The back is decorated with a painting of a ruined abbey in the Romantic tradition fostered by the literature of the early nineteenth century such as the novels of Sir Walter Scott. (Victoria & Albert Museum)

55 *above* Arm chair, ebonized beech with rush seat, produced from 1865 onwards by William Morris & Co and known as Sussex chairs. They were aimed at the customer of limited means as an alternative to the products of the usual commercial furniture manufacturer whose work was judged by Morris to be ill-designed and whose means of production were killing the craftsman's sense of achievement. (Victoria & Albert Museum)

every stage in a piece of furniture. In commercial furniture manufacture in the Victorian period, although there was little use of power machinery, division of labour was practised, and a man might find himself producing nothing but a certain type of chair leg. From the Arts and Crafts Movement, stimulated by the thought and enterprise of Morris, can be traced the road to modern functional design.

2 Tables

THE MAIN ROOM of a medieval house was the hall, and this room also featured prominently in most domestic buildings erected in Britain in the sixteenth century and the first half of the seventeenth. The hall was used in the Middle Ages for communal dining, the master and his family and guests sitting on a raised dais at one end and the servants and retainers in the body of the hall. The tables provided were often of trestle construction with stout elm tops. In the case of the well-known examples surviving at Penshurst Place in Kent, dating from the late fifteenth century, the tops are nearly 27½ feet long and are supported in each case by three massive oak pillar supports. Some trestle tables were designed to be dismantled should the full floor area of the hall be needed for some other social function.

In the late Middle Ages tables of framed construction were produced as an alternative to the earlier trestle type. These retained their popularity in the sixteenth century at a time when the trestle type had declined in importance. The Tudor house with its greater standards of comfort was provided with its own dining parlour in which the owner of the house and his family dined apart from the servants and smaller tables were also needed, as the room was smaller. These were usually of oak, rectangular in shape, and supported at the corners by carved or turned legs which were connected by stretchers near to ground level. From the last quarter of the sixteenth century until *c.* 1620 the legs were formed in a most ornate fashion with great turned and carved bulbs resembling covered cups, the detail copied from design books of Flemish origin which were doing much in this period to introduce Renaissance detail into England. These bulbs were decorated either with acanthus leaf carving or deep gadroons (plates 56 and 57). The underframe or frieze of the table was either carved (plate 56) or inlaid with geometrical designs in such woods as bog oak and

56 *top* Draw-table, oak, *c.* 1600, with gadroon carving on frieze and acanthus carving and gadroons on the bulbs. (Mallett)

57 *above* Draw-table, oak with inlaid frieze, *c.* 1600. The bulbs on the legs have carved gadrooning and the stretchers scratch mouldings. (Spink)

58 *left* Gate-leg table, oak, *c.* 1640, with carved frieze, baluster-turned legs and ground shelf. (Spink)

59 left Side table, oak, bearing the carved date 1677. A storage well is provided under the top and the front carved with the initials of the owner and a lunette border. (Geffrye Museum)

60 below Gate-leg dining table, oak, *c.*1670, with two gates and flaps and bobbin-turned legs and stretchers. (Hotspur)

holly (plate 57). Some of these tables incorporate two leaves that drew out to extend the length of the table (plate 56). This type of table known as the 'draw' or 'drawing' table, appears to have originated on the continent of Europe, first appearing in England *c.* 1550.

Apart from these large dining tables a whole range of smaller ancillary tables were made in the sixteenth century and the first half of the seventeenth, mainly in oak. Small tables incorporating the gate-leg principle were not uncommon in the seventeenth century. The example in plate 58 has baluster-shaped legs of simple design turned on a pole lathe and probably dates from the middle of the seventeenth century. The jointing is the almost ubiquitous mortice and tenon secured with wooden dowels. A single gate at the rear swings out to support the semi-circular flap that otherwise folds flat onto the fixed half of the top. Other small tables had a top that was hinged to reveal beneath a box that could be used for storage (plate 59). Although the example shown bears the date 1677, the characteristic lunette carving on the front and the simple baluster-turned leg could have been used on a similar table fifty years earlier. In country areas craftsmen continued to produce traditional oak furniture at least to the end of the seventeenth century, despite the fact that it had long ceased to be fashionable in London and other large urban centres. Small tables would find numerous uses. Some were possibly used as games tables, card games such as primero, gleek, maw and sant enjoying considerable popularity. Although nearly all tables that now survive are of oak and, apart from carving, relatively plain, inventory references of the period indicate that tables of walnut, some with imported marble tops of intricate design, once existed in the houses of the wealthy. One such example with an oak frame is to be seen in the long gallery at Aston Hall in Birmingham.

The old joiner tradition of the first half of the seventeenth century was carried into the second in the form of larger gate-leg tables that in many households took over from the framed table as dining tables (plate 60). Tops are either oval or round and two flaps with supporting gates were usual. Larger sizes exist with double gates at each end. The gates and legs provided opportunities for elaborate bobbin or twist turning. The larger type of gate-leg table enjoyed only a short period of popularity, for already by the Restoration period the habit of having a number of smaller tables instead of one large dining table was gaining popularity. With a few exceptions the large dining table did not reappear until the last decade of the eighteenth century.

The table most associated with the late Stuart period had a rectangular top supported by legs, often of twist turning. The legs are connected by flat, sinuous, X-shaped stretchers (plates 61 and 63). Table tops became elaborate and provided a surface that could be veneered in walnut, olive or laburnam. Particularly popular was 'oyster' parquetry work. A branch was cut transversely to provide a succession of veneers each of which repeated the circular grain pattern and these were used to cover the table top, matching pieces of veneer filling the spaces between. The effect was relieved by the use of circles and ovals of holly wood stringing (plate 62). Such parquetry was often used as a surround to a central panel of mar-

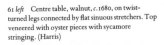

61 *left* Centre table, walnut, *c*.1680, on twist-turned legs connected by flat sinuous stretchers. Top veneered with oyster pieces with sycamore stringing. (Harris)

62 *below* Close-up of part of the table top in plate 61 showing the oyster veneer.

63 *bottom* Centre table, scagliola on pine carcase, *c*. 1680. Although the main centre for the supply of scagliola at this period was Italy, and particularly the city of Florence, the design and execution of this piece would suggest Dutch origin. (Victoria & Albert Museum)

64 *opposite* Table top of scagliola from the table shown in plate 63.

quetry in brightly contrasting woods, usually displaying vases of flowers. The effect was made more dramatic by the use of bone or sycamore stained green to represent the leaves. Such marquetry is in the tradition of Dutch design and no doubt was introduced into England by continental craftsmen who sought the patronage of the court of the restored Charles II, who had in 1660 set out from Holland at the end of his exile. A few tables were produced at this period with tops made from scagliola, a composition material consisting of plaster of Paris, into which marble chippings, alabaster, gypsum and so on are worked in imitation of marble. This technique enabled tops to be constructed with complex designs and pictures. The table in plate 63 has a top probably of Dutch manufacture worked with a complex pattern of flowers, birds and insects in scagliola (plate 64). The earliest recorded use of this material in England is in a fire surround in Ham House in Surrey, which is dated between 1673 and 1675. The table illustrated has distinct similarities to this work and must date from the same period.

Direct trade by sea between Europe and the Far East had been opened up by the Portuguese at the end of the fifteenth century, and by the beginning of the seventeenth the merchants of Holland, France and Britain had laid claim to a share of this trade. One of the off-shoots of this commerce was the importation as curiosities of pieces of oriental lacquer furniture, produced in China and Japan. English patrons in the reign of James I, Lord

65 *above* Games table, japanned, *c.*1700, with
folding top and two hinged supports. The shaped
baluster-turned legs are typical of the period.
(Mallett)

66 *below* Side table, carved and gilded limewood
with a marble top, *c.*1680. Carved work in the style
of Grinling Gibbons. (Spink)

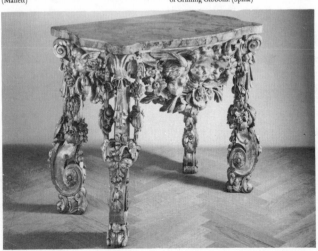

Northampton for example, are known to have owned such pieces. The great vogue for lacquered furniture however developed after the restoration of Charles II and its popularity resulted in attempts to produce imitation lacquer in England. Such imitation lacquer work is said to be japanned. Backgrounds used are usually black or red, though blue, green and buff are also known. The oriental landscapes and figures are raised and finished in gilt. Japanned work was particularly popular from c. 1680 to 1720 and the art was stimulated in 1688 by the publication of a handbook by John Stalker and George Parker entitled a *Treatise of Japanning and Varnishing* giving instructions on methods to be used and some designs for pseudo-oriental details. The table in plate 65 is a small card table. Two gates swing out at the back to support the semi-circular flap, which in the photograph is shown folded back on the table top. Such tables were also produced in walnut and sometimes equipped with little drawers in the frieze.

Another art developed in late Stuart England with the help of European craftsmen was gilding. The name most closely associated with its introduction is Jean Pelletier, a carver and gilder of French extraction who was active in England from c. 1690 to 1710 and was one of a number of foreign furniture craftsmen working in England at this period under the patronage of the court. This influx of skilled craftsmen from the continent Europe into England started well before the revocation of the Edict of Nantes in 1685 and resulted in a rapid advance in the standards of furniture making in all but provincial areas. Gilt furniture was produced for the state rooms of the late Stuart town and country houses. Like the interior decoration of these houses they reflect the arrival of the Baroque tradition in England. Heavily carved underframes were popular c. 1680 in the style of Grinling Gibbons, prominently displaying cherubs' heads, swags of flowers, fruit and foliage and also birds. Many tables, like the example in plate 66, had a marble top. Such tables were often decorated on the front and two sides to stand against a wall (side tables) but were sometimes decorated on all sides (centre tables). By c. 1700 the taste in gilt tables had changed and rectangular wooden tops were finished in raised gesso work (coats of whiting and size applied to wood work, then carved and gilded) and displayed intricate scroll patterns; they often incorporated the cyphers of the patrons. The florid style of the legs and stretchers derives from continental designers such as Jean Berain and Daniel Marot (plate 67). In England this style of table is associated with James Moore (fl. 1708–26) who supplied similar pieces to the royal household and other wealthy patrons.

By the end of the seventeenth century a wide range of tables had de-

67 *above* Side table, carved and gilt, *c*.1700. The
foliated scroll work top, gadrooned frieze and leg
capitals, and vase finial at the intersection of the
stretchers are features typical of this period. (Mallett)

68 *below* Writing table, japanned, *c*.169⟨
tapering necked legs with ball feet. (Mall⟨

veloped to serve specialist needs. Some were purely decorative, designed as part of the formal interior of the Baroque reception rooms of country and town houses by such architects as Sir Christopher Wren, Sir John Vanbrugh and William Talman (plates 66 and 67). Others were more functional, such as the lacquered writing table (plate 68) with its matching series of drawers either side of a central well of similar form to the knee-hole desk. Most functional tables produced by urban cabinet-makers were in walnut which might be used in the solid for both legs and top though the latter might alternatively be veneered. The small centre table in plate 69 clearly satisfied an entirely different need from that of the writing table, in plate 68 though both tables show common stylistic features of the period. An examination of the legs will show that they taper and are necked at the top. In both tables they end in ball feet and the legs are connected by flat but sinuous stretchers.

The Queen Anne period saw the introduction of the cabriole leg to tables, which were mainly to feature this form with various modifications until c. 1760. After the Hanoverian succession the knees were carved with acanthus leaf (plate 70) or shell motifs (plate 72) and terminated in ball and claw feet as with contemporary chairs. Deep aprons of sinuous outline were common under the table frieze (plates 70 and 71). A new form of card table is particularly associated with this early Georgian period (plate 72). The earlier types of card table with gate-leg action presented those seated around with an untidy collection of legs and stretchers on which they could catch their legs. The new type was hinged half-way down the side and opened by means of a concertina action so that when the table was both closed and open there was a leg at each corner. When the concertina frame had been extended, the top would be folded down on it to reveal a baize playing surface with polished wells for coins and counters. The popularity of this type of table is a reflection of the mania for gambling at cards indulged in by both men and women.

By the late 1720s carving on knees and frieze was becoming more pronounced under the influence of the Baroque interiors designed by the architect William Kent. Walnut was beginning to fall from fashion by the 1730s, giving way to mahogany. Typical of this phase is the table in plate 73. The lion mask carved on the knee, the crisp carving of the paw feet and the Vitruvian scroll border on the frieze are typical of the style associated with Kent. The tops of side tables designed for decorative effect were often of marble or scagliola, but in a number of cases classical mosaics were brought from Italy, possibly as a trophy of the Grand Tour. Gilding was favoured for both side tables (plates 71 and 74) and console tables

47

69 *left* Centre table, walnut, *c.*1690, with tapering turned legs and shaped stretchers. (Mallett)

70 *above* Dressing table, walnut, *c.*1730, with shaped underframe and cabriole legs, the knee carved with acanthus and terminating in ball and claw feet. (Mallett)

71 *below* Side table, carved and gilt, *c.*1720. The top and frieze are decorated with acanthus scrolling and the legs in cabriole form terminate in paw and ball feet. (Mallett)

72 right Card table, walnut, *c.* 1720, on cabriole legs terminating in ball and claw feet and with shell motifs carved on the knee. The top has dished areas for candlesticks at the four corners and wells for counters. (Mallett)

73 below Side table, carved and gilded with marble top, *c.* 1740. The frieze is carved with Vitruvian scroll; the cabriole legs, with lion masks carved on the knees, end in paw and ball feet. (Harris)

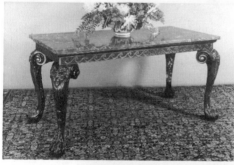

74 right Side table, carved and gilded with a marble top, *c.* 1745, decorated with a mask in the centre of the frieze and swags of foliage. The cabriole legs terminate in scrolls faced with satyr masks. (Mallett)

75 *above* Console table, carved and gilded with marble top, *c.*1730. The top is supported by an eagle seated on a rock. In the taste of William Kent. (Mallett)

76 *below* Side table, carved and gilded with marble top, *c.*1735. The frieze is supported at the front by two eagles and connected by swags to a central lion mask. A lower gadrooned border supports a central shell motif. In the taste of William Kent. (Mallett)

(plate 75). Swags of foliage and centre motifs in the form of human or animal masks (plates 74 and 76) decorate the frieze. With console tables that were designed to be fixed to a wall pier under a mirror, conventional legs might be dispensed with and the marble table tops were sometimes supported by eagles (plate 75) or dolphins.

Decorative gilt tables of this type provided an ideal field for Rococo influence, which was beginning to affect English taste soon after 1740. The style originated in France as a reaction to the heaviness of the formal Baroque style associated with Versailles and the court of Louis XIV. Rococo influence is clearly to be seen, for instance, in the table in plate 77. The heavy formality of the tables in the Kent taste has gone in favour of the light framework of C and S scroll work with a rhythm of form and movement that has been compared to the restless sea. Tables of this form are illustrated by Thomas Chippendale in the first edition of his *Director* (1754) and by William Ince and John Mayhew in their *Universal System* (1762) where they are described as 'frames for marble slabs'. Associated with the Chippendale period are tripod tea tables (plate 78). These have either a round or rectangular top with a raised pie-crust edge or a fretted gallery to prevent the tea bowls and other porcelain from being swept off accidentally. The top rests on a 'birdcage' that enables it to be revolved, or pivoted in a vertical plane for ease of storage. Despite the high price of tea, the habit of tea drinking had become almost universal in upper-class and middle-class society by the middle of the eighteenth century and by the end of the century was even indulged in by many of the lower classes. Similar round tables are known, the tops of which are dished to receive a number of plates. These are usually known as supper tables. Rectangular tables with similar raised and fretted rims exist from this period (plate 79) and are described by Chippendale in his *Director* as 'china tables'. They probably served a function similar to that of the tripod type but of course had a larger capacity.

An ingenious table showing subdued Rococo influence in its shaping is illustrated in plate 80. This was probably intended as a ladies' writing table but was also provided at the back with a screen covered with pleated silk that could be raised to protect the face from the heat of a fire. This type of table enjoyed a period of considerable popularity and a version was illustrated by Thomas Sheraton in his *Drawing Book* (1791–4).

The influence of Robert Adam and neo-classicism on furniture design from the 1760s led to the adoption of simpler outlines to tables. One of the most common types of table of this Adam/Hepplewhite period is the half-round side or card table (plate 81). Legs are straight and tapered, some-

77 *above* Console table, carved and gilded with a
marble top, *c.*1750, with two scrolled cabriole
supports and a shell motif supported by the
stretchers. This table shows distinct Rococo
influence in the fanciful use of scroll work and shell
motifs. (Mallett)

78 *left* Tea table, mahogany, *c.*1750, with tripod
stand terminating in ball and claw feet and with
carved acanthus decoration. (Hotspur)

79 *below* Tea or china table, mahogany,
*c.*1760, on square-section legs with block feet
and fret brackets between legs and frieze.
(Mallett)

times ending in spade feet. Carving is little used as decoration and in its place marquetry work and banding with other woods are adopted. By this period the dense 'Spanish' mahogany from San Domingo, which showed little grain, had been replaced by Cuban and Honduras types with much more attractive grain pattern and range of shades.

Another type of table that reached its zenith of popularity in the last quarter of the eighteenth century was the Pembroke table (plate 82). This type was known to Chippendale, who described basically similar ones in the *Director* as 'breakfast tables'. Examples of the 1760s, however, usually have diagonal stretchers between the legs. The Pembroke table is said to have received its name from the Countess of Pembroke, who according to Thomas Sheraton was the first patron to order this type of table. It consists of a centre section with a long drawer beneath, and a flap at each side supported on brackets that swing out from the centre section. With the flaps raised the surface area of the table is in most cases doubled as each flap is half the width of the centre section. The legs, which are usually straight and tapered, often end in castors that enabled the table to be moved about the room as required. The drawers on most Pembroke tables are fitted with two handles with pressed brass plates or cast brass knobs and a similar pair are to be found on the false drawer front at the other end. Pembroke tables could be used as breakfast tables and also as writing tables; one version, the 'harlequin' Pembroke table was equipped with a set of drawers and compartments for writing materials that ingeniously rose from a well in the table when required. Most Pembroke tables are in mahogany, but a number were produced in satinwood with painted decoration. Some tables had shaped tops, elaborate banding and marquetry work. Small, high-quality Pembroke tables are very much sought after.

Throughout most of the eighteenth century large dining tables were out of fashion and a number of small tables were brought into the room at meal times. Thus Chippendale and other mid-eighteenth-century designers do not illustrate dining tables, though they were made in small numbers. By the 1790s, however, they were once more commonly in production. A popular type consisted of two half-round ends supported on tripod bases between which additional sections could be inserted (plate 83). An equally popular form was a table with a round top on a pillar support and claws. The top tilted into an upright position for storage and carriage (plate 84). Round tables long remained popular and were common in the middle of the nineteenth century. A variant of the round-topped table designed to take leaves to extend its size was the capstan table (plate 85). This was patented in 1835 by the London cabinet-makers Johnstone,

80 *above* Ladies' writing table, mahogany with top cross-banded, *c.*1770. The cabriole legs and general shaping is French in inspiration. A screen of pleated silk is fitted at the back which may be raised to provide protection against the heat of a fire. (Harris)

81 *above left* Card table, mahogany with banded top and marquetry paterae at the tops of the square-section tapering legs, *c.*1785. (Mallett)

82 *left* Pembroke table, mahogany, *c.*1780 on square-section, tapering legs carved with strings of husks and paterae at frieze level. (Mallett)

83 *below* Dining table, mahogany, *c.*1795, made in sections each supported on a turned column ending in four curved legs. (Mallett)

84 *above* Dining table, mahogany with top cross-banded, *c.*1800, on central support with four reeded legs. (Mallett)

85 *below* Capstan dining table, mahogany, *c.*1840, shown in its fully expanded form. The top is supported by one centre and four supplementary turned columns, terminating on a deep plinth. (Harris)

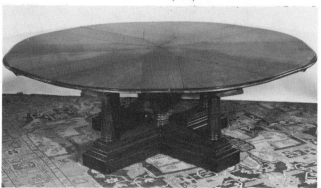

Jupe & Co.

The Regency period produced various new types of table. One of the most attractive was the set of quartetto tables (plate 86). These tables were of graduated heights and size so that they would store under one another. This type of table is described by Thomas Sheraton in his *Cabinet Dictionary* (1803) and appears to belong mainly to the first decades of the nineteenth century. They must have proved particularly useful in the more limited space available in middle-class town houses and their relatively short-lived period of production is therefore difficult to explain. This type of table appeals to the house furnisher of today and has been much reproduced in recent years.

Styling of Regency tables, and furniture generally, was much affected by the influence of the art connoisseur and amateur architect Thomas Hope. His attempts to design furniture for his own house in Duchess Street, London, which housed his collection of ancient and classical art, led him to study and adapt furniture forms and detail used in classical times. The example of the copying of the Greek *klismos* and its effect on Greek chair design has already been noted (see p. 32). Tables also show Hope's influence. They are supported on animal monopodia (an animal's head supporting the table top, and the table leg in the form of the chest, leg and paw of the animal) (plate 87). Other tables are supported by X-frame (plate 88) or lyre supports at the ends, again based on forms used in the classical world.

Brass embellishments and stringing are common and brass inlay is found on both table tops and supports (plate 90). Circular tables using a central pillar support become common and the table shown in plate 90, though rather later in date, is clearly based upon a design illustrated in Thomas Hope's *Household Furniture and Interior Decoration* (1807). A table of similar shape was made for Hope's London house.

Games tables were popular in the Regency period and often incorporated a well in the centre for backgammon (plate 89). When not in use such wells were often covered by a sliding panel marked out with a chessboard. The example in plate 89 is supported on slim, turned legs decorated with raised rings. Similar types of legs are not unusual on tables of Sheraton and early Regency date, (usually post 1800) as the popularity of the tapered, square-section Hepplewhite period leg waned.

Another type of table that developed during the Regency was the sofa table. This is usually long and narrow with flaps supported by brackets at each end to extend the table if required. The end supports, each with two splayed feet, are connected by a stretcher rail (plate 91), though in other

86 *left* Set of 'quartetto' tables, mahogany, *c.*1810, on slender turned supports with the edge of the tops reeded. (Mallett)

87 *below* Writing table, mahogany, *c.*1810, with the two front supports in the form of lion monopodia. In the taste of Thomas Hope. (Mallett)

88 *below* Writing table, rosewood, *c.*1810, on X-frame supports. The applied metal mounts on the frieze are in the form of palmette decoration at the corners, inverted anthemion motifs for the keyhole escutcheons and star bolt heads to act as drawer pulls. (Mallett)

examples a centre support is used. Such tables, as the name suggests, were designed to stand beside a sofa to facilitate drawing, writing or reading. Their size, utility, attractiveness of form and finish make them an item in considerable demand today and as a consequence prices are high.

Although they are known at an earlier date, rent tables (plate 92) are particularly distinctive of the Regency period. They are circular in shape and have a series of drawers in the frieze, which are often lettered. The top of the table usually revolves. Such tables are normally of considerable size and were used in the collection of rent from tenants on large country estates and in business premises. Another type of table that utilized a round top was one form of Regency library table. Here a row of bookshelving was incorporated in the deep frieze. Drum tables of all kinds are distinctive of the Regency period.

For the reception rooms of large houses giltwood furniture returned to fashion in the Regency period. Particularly associated with the naval victories of Nelson was the use of dolphin supporters (plate 93). One of the finest suites of furniture featuring this theme is the Greenwich Hospital suite presented by the widow of Mr John Fish in 1813 for use in the reception rooms at this naval hospital in gratitude for the success achieved by Lord Nelson. The suite is now on display at the Royal Pavilion in Brighton.

By the Regency period the Gothic style of architecture had become an accepted alternative to the normal classical styles. The main Regency architects such as Wyatt, Smirke and Nash worked in both, and George IV used Sir Jeffrey Wyatville to carry out an extensive programme of building in this style at Windsor Castle. It is thus not surprising that Gothic furniture featured in Regency design books. Gothic form in architecture was better understood than it had been in the mid-eighteenth century when Horace Walpole popularized the style in the work that he carried out at Strawberry Hill, Twickenham (Middlesex). A true appreciation of Gothic craftsmanship and design still eluded designers in the Regency period however and this is seen very clearly in the Gothic furniture produced. Gothic decorative motifs and weak tracery were used to disguise pieces of furniture that in basic form differed little from the furniture produced in the usual 'Grecian' style (plate 94).

A much more serious attempt to capture the spirit of Gothicism both in construction and detail is to be seen in the table designed by the Victorian architect A. W. N. Pugin (plate 95). Both Pugin and his father, who had been an assistant to the Regency architect John Nash, had published books of furniture designs in the Gothic style, but only those of the son really

89 *left* Games table, mahogany with boxwood stringing, *c.*1810. The table is supported on four slender turned legs and the well is marked out with a backgammon board. (Mallett)

90 *right* Centre table, rosewood, *c.*1820, on central concave-sided pedestal. The base, pedestal and edge of the top are decorated with brass inlay. The shape of the table is based on one designed by Thomas Hope for his Duchess Street house. (Harris)

91 *left* Sofa table, rosewood, *c.*1810, supported on turned standards, splayed at the foot and ending in castors. The top has an edge banding of brass inlay. (Mallett)

59

92 *above* Rent table, mahogany, *c*.1800. The centre of the top has a concealed compartment and the cupboard base is fitted with shelves. (Mallett)

93 *right* Games table with inlaid marble top supported on carved and gilt dolphins and with ball and claw feet, *c*.1820. (Mallett)

94 *below* Writing table, gilt and ebonized and in Gothic taste, *c*.1820. (Mallett)

attempt to recapture an honesty of construction and design that is medieval in spirit. By the 1840s A. W. N. Pugin was designing for J. G. Crace & Son and he was responsible for the design of furniture for the new Houses of Parliament, for which he was also employed in producing architectural designs. By the 1850s and 1860s Gothic form and detail were having a very pronounced effect on design generally, though in the secular field they always represented a minority taste. A number of commercial producers did however take up the style, and it was of paramount importance in influencing the work of William Morris and the Arts and Crafts Movement. In the commercial field it helped to popularize a revival in the use of oak for fashionable furniture and provided a vehicle for the revival of the art of the carver.

After 1830, however, the main prevailing style until well after the middle of the century was the 'Grecian' which had been popularized in the Regency period. Thus there is no clear-cut watershed in 1830 and it is often difficult to distinguish between late Regency and early Victorian furniture in this style. Attempts by the antique trade to talk about 'William IV' furniture only cloud the issue further, for no distinctive style was developed during the short, seven-year reign of this king. All that it is possible to say is that the 'Grecian' forms popular in the Regency in many cases continued to be made after 1830 for many years, though with late Regency and early Victorian examples the amount of carved decoration increased and the proportions tended to become heavier. The table in plate 96 with its four claws and centre support owes much to Regency design, but the lobes at the top of the legs with their carved acanthus and the heavy turning of the centre support betray a Victorian rather than a Georgian date.

Tables with a round and later hexagonal top were favoured and were generally referred to as loo tables, after a card game of that name. Side and card tables were however often D-shaped, the table top on the latter being pivoted so that when the full area of the top was required it could be swung at right angles to its normal position and both the flap and table top would be supported on the well beneath the top. By c. 1850 the sturdy central column support had been replaced by a platform from which arose a cluster of four slender supports. Victorian tables are found in mahogany, rosewood and walnut, those in the last wood sometimes incorporating fine floral marquetry in their tops. Pembroke tables with much more sturdy legs continued to be made, but the elegance of late eighteenth-century examples had been lost and a version with a very narrow top and two large flaps became known as the Sutherland table; it was used in smaller rooms.

95 *above* Centre table, carved walnut with inlaid top designed by A. W. N. Pugin and made in 1847 by J. G. Crace for Abney Hall, Cheshire. (Victoria & Albert Museum)

96 *right* Side table, rosewood, *c.* 1840, with folding top and well beneath. The turned support ends in four claws with acanthus carving on the lobed knees. The rosewood tea caddy is of similar date. (Private collection)

97 *left* Work-table, satinwood banded with other woods, *c.*1790. The lid lifts to reveal compartments for needles, cottons, etc., while the bag beneath holds work in progress. (Harris)

98 *above* Designs for work-tables with
hexagonal tops and bell-shaped bodies from plate
LVII of *The Cabinet-Maker's Assistant* (1853).

WORK TABLES

Work tables were produced from *c*. 1770 with a fitted compartment beneath the top and below that a pouch that could be slid out; in this pouch work in progress could be kept (plate 97). This type of table is particularly associated with the Regency period but was also produced in the early Victorian period. A much more common type in the mid-Victorian period had a cone-shaped body supported on a base or claws (plate 98). This type was usually executed in walnut. Work tables often doubled as game tables and are frequently found with a chessboard on the top.

3 Storage and Display Furniture

THE NEED to store possessions unwanted at a particular moment, or the desire to display to admiring guests items of value, rarity or interest, have resulted in the development of an extensive range of different pieces of furniture, which are described in this chapter.

CHESTS

In the Middle Ages these functions were fulfilled by the chest. One of the best places to look for medieval chests today is in old parish churches, where they have for many centuries served as receptacles for vestments, church plate and parish documents. In their crudest form they consisted of tree trunks hollowed out and provided with a rudimentary lid. By the thirteenth century lighter chests were made, consisting of boards nailed or dowelled together to form a box that was raised off the damp floor by extending the end boards to form short legs. This simple type of boarded chest, the work of the carpenter, was to continue to be made in country areas until the beginning of the eighteenth century from native timbers, the most common of which was oak. Some medieval examples are elaborately carved, while from the late sixteenth century the date and initials of the owner are often carved on the front, a practice common on many different pieces of furniture in this period. The boarded chest although simple to construct, made no allowance for movement in the timber, and shrinkage and warpage could result in the boards splitting away from the nails or dowels used for jointing.

By the fifteenth century a new type of construction was being employed which involved a framework, secured with mortice and tenon joints, to hold panels chamfered on the edges to fit in grooves provided on the frame members. The mortice and tenon was in each case held in position by a dowelling pin through the joint (see figure 3). This joined type of construction was to be almost universally employed in the fashionable furniture produced up to *c.* 1660 in London and other urban centres, and after this date was still the usual construction in country areas for the next fifty years. A craftsman of greater skill than the carpenter was required for this type of construction, and furniture involving mortice and tenon joints was the province of members of the joiners' guilds. Most of the chests that survive are of late sixteenth- and seventeenth-century date. Plate 99 shows a chest of *c.* 1600 with arcaded front panels, each carved arch providing a surround for an inlaid floral pattern and the whole conception showing strong Renaissance influence. The carved lozenges on the ends are a motif very common in furniture produced *c.* 1600 and the decades that immediately followed. Plate 100 shows the same arcading on the front but it is less architectural. Because it was made a few years later the inlay is absent and a stylized floral pattern is carved instead.

Foreign craftsmanship was much admired during the sixteenth century and was acknowledged to be finer than that available from English craftsmen. A result of this was the importation of the work of foreign furniture craftsmen on a considerable scale under the influence of court patronage. Both Henry VIII and Cardinal Wolsey had their agents on the Continent for this purpose. Continental influence can also be seen in furniture pro-

Figure 3. Front of joined chest to show frame and panel type of construction.

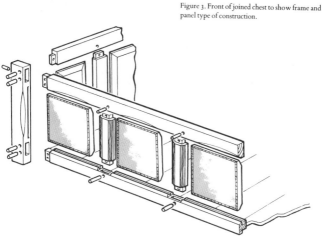

99 *left* Chest of panelled construction, oak with inlays of other woods, *c*. 1600. (Harris)

100 *right* Chest of panelled construction, oak, first half of the seventeenth century. Arcaded front with carved foliage decoration. (Harris)

101 *below* Chest, oak with inlays of holly and bog oak, *c*.1600, probably made by immigrant German craftsmen in a style similar to that used in the Cologne area of Germany at that time. (Victoria & Albert Museum)

duced in England, particularly in some chests of late sixteenth-century date decorated with elaborate inlay and mouldings of an architectural nature (plate 101). Such pieces have in the past been called 'Nonsuch chests' but it is quite clear that the building featured in the inlay work is not the Palace of Nonsuch (Cleam, Surrey), a favourite haunt of Elizabeth I, and that the workmanship closely resembles similar work produced in the Cologne area of Germany at the period. There is reason to believe that these chests are the work of immigrant German workers in England and that the centre of their trade was in Southwark.

From the late sixteenth century some chests incorporating drawers in their base were produced; from their hybrid nature these are referred to as mule chests. Such pieces became more common in the early seventeenth century and plate 102 shows an example of such a composite piece, in this case with no fewer than five drawers. Mule chests continued to be made into the mid-eighteenth century but, as with chests, their popularity was very much on the decline from the mid-seventeenth century when chests of drawers became more popular.

Chests of a decorative nature did, however, continue to be produced in limited quantities. From the 1720s a number of carved gilt chests in sarcophagus form were made to suit the Baroque style of interior favoured by William Kent. Another type favoured in the eighteenth century was the lacquered chest on a stand. Some of the chests were imported from Canton in ships of European East India Companies and provided with

102 *left* Chest, with drawers in lower section, oak, *c.*1650. The upper section is the chest compartment. (Harris)

103 *above* Chest, red lacquer on japanned stand, *c*.1720. (Mallett)

104 *right* Chest of drawers, oak, late seventeenth century, with applied split baluster decoration and mouldings. (Harris)

stands of European manufacture. Others were equally certainly products of the japanner, using different materials and techniques. In England japanned furniture was produced in considerable quantity in the period from c. 1680 and those engaged in the trade were sufficiently influential to petition Parliament as early as 1692 to obtain a ban on the importation of lacquer from the East. A typical early eighteenth-century lacquer chest is shown in plate 103; this displays the elaborate chased lockplates used on lacquered furniture in this period.

CHESTS OF DRAWERS

Storage of small items of clothing in chests was obviously inconvenient and by the end of the sixteenth century drawers were beginning to appear in furniture, as for example in the mule chest. At first drawers were called 'tills' or 'drawing boxes' and were of very crude construction. It is clear, however, from an agreement made between the Joiners' and Carpenters' Companies of London in 1632 that the former were already familiar with the dovetail joint. At first the pins used on dovetails holding the drawer front to the sides were large and crude (figure 4) but by the reign of Charles II finer and more even dovetailing had been adopted for fashionable furniture. The chest of drawers was merely an extension of the practice first applied with the mule chest, but it was not a commonly used

Figure 4. Drawer of c. 1680 showing a crude early form of dovetail joint much used in the first half of the seventeenth century (probably provincial craftsmanship).

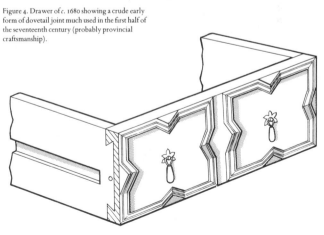

105 *right* Chest of drawers, walnut with marquetry panels, *c.*1680. The floral marquetry is Dutch in inspiration. (Spink)

106 *right* Chest of drawers, walnut, late seventeenth century, with drawers of different depths. The pear-shaped pulls on the drawer fronts are typical of this period. (Spink)

piece of furniture until the Restoration. A number of chests of drawers that exist from the period before 1660 had doors to cover the drawer fronts.

Chests of drawers from c. 1650 and especially those of the early years of Charles II's reign were often elaborately decorated with applied geometric or architectural mouldings, an influence coming from German, Dutch or Flemish sources. The chest of drawers illustrated in plate 104 is of this period, though the bracket feet on which it stands are of a later date. The sides of the chest are still of panelled construction and the front is decorated with applied split baluster decoration, a form introduced in the pre-Restoration period. The geometric mouldings stand out boldly from the drawer fronts. The top drawer is deep, reflecting the development from the composite mule chests with their opening lid to the chest section at the top. Plate 106 shows a chest of the same period but with simpler mouldings. It retains the bun feet common in this period and has a narrow drawer at the top reminiscent of similar drawers found in the friezes of cabinets of this period. Some seventeenth-century chests of drawers are made in two sections for ease of movement.

At roughly the same time as the return of Charles II from exile in 1660 considerable advances in furniture construction took place. In fashionable furniture the frame and panel type of construction, which had been almost universal for two hundred years, was replaced by case construction. A carcase, usually of pine or oak, was constructed by means of dovetails and this in its turn was veneered, normally in this period in walnut. Contemporary with the introduction of veneering was the use of marquetry, exploiting the different colours of woods to form a picture or pattern in the veneer (figure 5). Such advances in workmanship must be associated with the introduction by foreign craftsmen of new techniques developed on the Continent.

A strong Dutch influence is to be seen in the floral marquetry that was used from c. 1670 to decorate many pieces of furniture. Such marquetry is usually contained within well-defined panels of curved outline (plate 105). At first, as on the example illustrated, the marquetry was in the form of sprays of tulips and carnations using a wide range of marquetry woods and also stained bone to simulate the green of the leaves. Later work shows a more restrained repertoire of marquetry woods and by the end of the century complicated arabesques, usually referred to as endive or seaweed marquetry, were in favour.

Marquetry was out of favour at the beginning of the eighteenth century. Chests of drawers veneered in walnut were, however, far from

107 Chest of drawers, walnut, c.1690. The top is cross-banded and there are bands of feathering on the edges of drawer fronts which are graduated in size. (Mallett)

108 Chest of drawers on stand, oak with banded drawer fronts, c.1700. The drawers are graduated in size and the arcaded stand on turned tapered legs has three drawers in it following the usual pattern at this period. (Hotspur)

109 Chest on chest (tallboy), burr walnut with inlaid and concave sunburst on lowest drawer front, c.1710. (Harris)

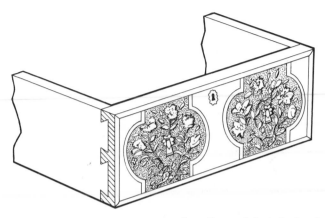

Figure 5. Drawer *c.* 1680 showing finer dovetails
(London or fine provincial craftsmanship).

plain, as full advantage was taken of the figure of the wood to gain pleasing effects. The top of the chest of drawers shown in plate 107 is a good
example of the practice of quartering the top—using four adjacent veneers from a piece of figured walnut and matching the grain pattern. The
borders of the drawers show feathering—the matching of two thin pieces
of walnut veneer to produce a chevron effect. Drawers of this period are
not fitted with cock-bead but a half-rounded moulding is applied to the
carcase between the drawers (figure 6). Some chests of the late seventeenth and early eighteenth centuries are provided with a writing surface
which folds flat on the top of the chest of drawers when not required.
Two lopers pull out from the chest to support the writing surface when in
use. Such chests of drawers are usually referred to as bachelor chests.

The inconvenience of reaching down to the bottom drawer resulted in
chests of drawers being constructed on stands. This practice is also found
with chests. These can usually be dated from the style of legs and stretchers
adopted for the stand. Those of the period of Charles II, for instance,
usually have stands incorporating baluster-turned or twist-turned legs. By
the time of William and Mary peg-top legs connected with flat stretchers
of sinuous outline were used (plate 108). Drawers were incorporated in
the stand. The peg-top leg with stretchers was in its turn replaced by the
cabriole leg, which is used on most early eighteenth-century chests of drawers on stands. By this period, however, a rival had arisen in the form of

73

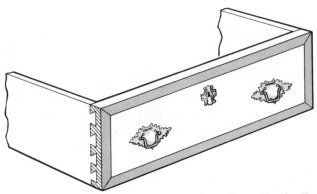

Figure 6. Drawer of c. 1715. Half-round moulding on the carcase between the drawers or lip mould fitted to the top of the drawer front.

the tallboy or chest on chest (plate 109). Although this piece of furniture had obvious advantages in its economical use of floor space, it must have proved inconvenient, because to reach the top drawers it might be necessary to stand on a chair. Nevertheless the tallboy had by c. 1730 taken over completely from the chest of drawers on stand, and was to retain its popularity until nearly the end of the century. Early Georgian examples have the drawer fronts finely veneered in burr walnut and cross-banded at the edges. Finer examples have fluted canted corners to the top section, and a marquetry sunburst in the centre of the bottom drawer which has a semi-circular recess to accommodate it (plate 109). They dismantle into two sections for ease of transportation. Early Georgian chests of drawers show many of the same features, such as the use of burr walnut and fluted canted corners (plate 110).

By c. 1740 mahogany was used as a veneer on chests of drawers and many relatively plain specimens like the one in plate 111, must have been produced during this period. Some chests of drawers and tallboys were fitted with slides, which provided a surface either for brushing clothes on or for writing. Japanned chests of drawers lacquered on a pine carcase are a feature of this period (c. 1750), when there was a revival of interest in Chinoiserie (plate 112). Rococo influence from France is clearly visible in the serpentine shape that was accepted for the finer chests of this period (plate 113). French influence is also to be seen in the shaping of the feet and

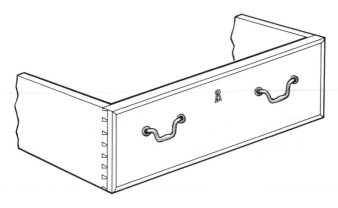

Figure 7. Drawer *c.* 1760.

the apron of the chest in plate 114. By *c.* 1770, however, the serpentine form was being rivalled by the bow-fronted chest, which conformed to the simpler outlines demanded by the neo-classical taste. An example is illustrated by George Hepplewhite in his *Guide*, though he also features the serpentine-fronted chest. The bow-fronted chest shown in plate 115 with its turned feet, cable-twist columns and oval draw plates is a fine example of Regency design, but the bow-fronted chest was to enjoy a long run of popularity and was still in production in the middle of Victoria's reign. From the late Regency period chests of drawers and other cabinet furniture were increasingly fitted with wooden knobs instead of brass plates. J. C. Loudon in his *Encyclopaedia* (1833) praised this practice, declaring that the wooden knobs 'harmonise better and do not tarnish'. The tendency in recent years has been to despise the use of wooden knobs and many Victorian chests have been fitted with reproduction brass plates to give them a superficially Georgian appearance. The continued use of mahogany and the relative lack of development in the design of chests of drawers in the early Victorian period makes this possible.

The use of serpentine and bow-fronted forms did not oust the straight-fronted chest, which continued to be produced in very considerable quantities in mahogany for the upper and middle classes and also in pine for working-class homes and for servants' rooms. Some late Victorian chests were provided with porcelain knobs as an alternative to the turned wooden ones.

110 *above*   Chest of drawers, walnut, *c.*1720, with canted and fluted corners and drawers graduated in size. (Mallett)

111 *above right*   Chest of drawers, mahogany, *c.*1740, on bracket feet and with brushing slide under top. Drawers edged with cock bead. (Mallett)

112 *right*   Chest of drawers, japanned, *c.*1750, on bracket feet. Drawers fitted with swan neck loop handles. (Mallett)

113 *below*   Chest of drawers, mahogany, *c.*1765, with serpentine front and canted fluted corners on deep plinth. (Hotspur)

114 *below right*   Chest of drawers, mahogany, *c.*1790, with serpentine front and splayed French feet and shaped apron between. Stamped brass plates used on drawer fronts (Mallett)

115 *right* Chest of drawers, mahogany, *c*.1810, bow fronted with spiral-twisted colonettes at the angles ending in turned feet. The drawers are fitted with pressed brass plates in the form of oval paterae. (Harris)

116 *left* Commode, serpentine shape in the French taste, *c*.1765, with banding and marquetry in various woods and decorated at the corners with ormolu mounts. (Mallett)

117 *right* Commode, satinwood with cross-banding in various woods, *c*.1785, on short tapering square-section legs. (Mallett)

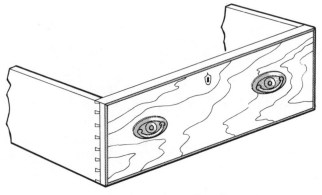

Figure 8. Drawer c. 1815.

COMMODES

A strong admiration for French furniture resulted in the introduction of the commode into England c. 1740. From then until the end of the century it was to have more care and attention lavished upon it than any other item of furniture, and was to form a vital part of the furnishing in late eighteenth-century reception rooms. Its function was the same as that of a chest of drawers or a cupboard, but the workmanship and decoration lavished upon it placed it in a class by itself. Leading cabinet-makers such as William Vile, Thomas Chippendale, John Cobb and Pierre Langlois are known to have produced commodes. These show strong French influence with their elaborate decoration and the extensive use of intricate ormolu mounts. Carving was used on examples until the 1760s, but then went out of fashion to a considerable degree. Two commodes at Osterley House in Middlesex are decorated with lacquer and have stylistic characteristics that point to the work of Thomas Chippendale who used the same finish on examples at Nostell Priory in Yorkshire. The fashion for commodes revived the art of marquetry. The example illustrated in plate 116 has marquetry panels of birds decorating the front, with floral marquetry on the sides. The serpentine shape is typical of the French Rococo taste and this is accentuated by the use of metal mounts of fine quality. Marquetry commodes in the same taste are known to have been made by John Cobb and Pierre Langlois.

The neo-classical taste popularized by the work of Robert Adam demanded simpler shaping, and half-round commodes on short tapering legs become the standard pattern (plate 117). These are often in satinwood with oval panels which allow painted decoration in the style of Angelica Kauffmann, an artist responsible for executing neo-classical painting for interior decoration schemes designed by Robert Adam. An alternative to painted decoration was marquetry work featuring typical Adam motifs such as classical urns, *amthemion* (honeysuckle), swags of husks or bell flowers and winged sphinxes.

By the last decade of the eighteenth century the commode had declined in importance in household furnishing schemes and later examples lack the elaborate shaping or carved, marquetry or painted decoration. The example illustrated in plate 118, although pleasing, appears to be more functional than decorative. During the Regency period the chiffonier was developed. This consisted of display or book shelves, often with a cupboard below and appears to have finally ousted the commode.

CHIFFONIERS

The term 'chiffonier' was used in 1808 by George Smith in his design book *Household Furniture* to describe a piece of furniture resembling a cupboard with open shelves for display purposes or for holding books. The pieces that he illustrates are clearly designed as important pieces of furnishing schemes and, like the commode, were intended to act as a focus of attention in a reception or drawing room. But by the 1820s the term was being applied to a narrow cupboard or cabinet with shelves above. A Regency rosewood chiffonier of this period is illustrated in plate 119. The turned columns flanking the cupboard, gadrooned edges to the top and shelves and scrolled supports to the upper shelf are typical features of chiffoniers of this period. Victorian examples are at times much larger with a cupboard closed by doors at the bottom, a marble top and mirror glass behind the shelves. This type is illustrated in *The Cabinet-maker's Assistant* (1853). A mid-Victorian example of a small chiffonier with a writing surface substituted at the top for the superstructure of display shelves is illustrated in plate 120.

CUPBOARDS

The term 'cupboard' is a generic one and can be used to cover most items of storage furniture except chests and chests of drawers. The word is not widely used in respect of a shelved piece of furniture covered by doors until the late seventeenth century. In the Middle Ages cupboards were

118 *above* Commode, harewood with bandings of other woods and a painted satinwood border on the top, *c*.1795. (Mallett)

119 *below* Chiffoniers, rosewood, *c*. 1820, with bookshelves below and display space above on deep plinth. (Mallett)

known as 'aumbries', and the usual term in the sixteenth century and early seventeenth was 'press'. Where the word cupboard is used in inventories in this period it describes a series of open shelves for the storage or display of drinking vessels or plate (quite literally a 'cup board') (see p. 86).

Oak cupboards of the period before 1660 exist in a number of forms. Some have pierced door fronts to allow ventilation and were clearly designed for the storage of food. In this form they are often referred to as dole or livery cupboards, though sixteenth and seventeenth-century inventory entries do not support the use of these terms for such cupboards. Because of their function a number of these cupboards were designed to hang from walls in order to protect the food from the attention of vermin. Plate 121 shows an example dating from c. 1600 with a front panel and cornice showing considerable architectural influence. The inlaid geometric design and chequer work is also typical of furniture of this date. Dole cupboards were not produced in any quantity after the first half of the seventeenth century.

For storage in hall and parlour in sixteenth- and early seventeenth-century houses elaborate framed cupboards (presses) were devised. Some were designed with upper and lower sections, the one at the top being shallower to allow a shelf in front. The example in plate 122 shows an elaborate version of this type of cupboard in which the top section incorporates a cupboard with the sides canted to allow display space. The bulbs on the supports for the cornice and the caryatid figures carved on the top cupboard are typical of the finer furniture of the late sixteenth century and are indications of strong influence from North German, Dutch or Flemish sources. The vine carving on the styles and bulbs and the floral inlay on the panels of the lower part of the cupboard are other features to be noted. This type of cupboard has many features in common with the court cupboard (see pp. 85–6).

The term buffet has been applied to cupboards of this type but there is no contemporary warrant for its use. Although cupboards of this type continued to be made after 1660, such manufacture was confined to country areas and examples are much less elaborate. Plain cupboards of similar style are known as late as the mid-eighteenth century from Wales, and were known as 'tridarns' or 'deuddarns' depending on whether they were constructed with three or two tiers or stages.

WARDROBES

The storage of clothing was facilitated by the development of the clothes press or wardrobe. Oak cupboards of frame and panel construction which

120 *right*
Chiffonier,
walnut, *c.*1860,
with leather
writing surface on
top. The inside of
the drawer bears
the stamped
inscription 'Made
· by Henry Ratty
Cabinet-Maker
Upholsterer 117 &
119 North Lane
Brighton'
(working at this
address 1856–64).
(Private
collection)

121 *right* Food
cupboard, oak,
*c.*1600, with
arcaded door inlaid
in geometrical
pattern and
chequer work, and
carved guilloche
border. (Spink)

122 *left*
Cupboard,
oak with inlay of
holly and bog oak
c.1590, with
strapwork pattern
on drawer front in
central frieze. The
canted cupboard in
the top half has
four caryatid
supporters. (Spink)

were clearly designed for the storage of clothes are known, but they do not appear to have been popular after 1660, when presumably the chest of drawers and the tallboy were thought sufficient. By the middle of the eighteenth century, however, the wardrobe was a very serious rival to the tallboy and a number of designs for such pieces appear in Chippendale's *Director* and other contemporary design books. Wardrobes of the late Georgian period usually consist of an upper section enclosed by two doors which cover a number of trays or shelves on which the folded clothes were stored. The lower section consists of a number of drawers (plate 123). Larger wardrobes followed a similar pattern but had flanking wings, usually slightly recessed, that provided space in which clothes could be hung. A fine example of this type is shown in plate 124. This is in the Gothic taste of the Regency period, which was stimulated by essays in architecture in this style by Wyatt, Nash, Smirke and Wyatville. Of the three wardrobe designs illustrated in J. C. Loudon's *Encyclopaedia* (1833) only two provide any space for hanging clothes and most of the storage is in the form of shelves. Many Victorian wardrobes, however, have doors extending down to ground level and mirror plates in the door. There is also a tendency in the second half of the nineteenth century for wardrobes to be provided only with hanging space and for the use of fitted shelves and trays to decline.

123 *left* Wardrobe, mahogany, c.1765, with four drawers in lower part and a cupboard fitted with trays in the upper. The wardrobe is mounted on ogee bracket feet and the cornice has a carved frieze of dentil moulding and arcading in the Gothic taste. (Mallett)

124 *left* Wardrobe, rosewood, c.1815, in Gothic taste. This piece is of a break-front type with provision for hanging clothes in the two wing cupboards. (Victoria & Albert Museum)

CABINETS AND DISPLAY FURNITURE

One of the earliest pieces of furniture designed purely for display was the court cupboard, which was associated particularly with the period of the reign of Elizabeth I. This consisted of open shelves, usually two in number, designed to display plate and cups though in some cases a cupboard with canted sides incorporated in the top half is known (plate 125). In wealthy households plate would be of gold or silver, in the houses of yeomen or tradesmen probably of pewter. Most of the court cupboards that survive are of late sixteenth- or early seventeenth-century date and are elaborately decorated with carving or inlay. This type of furniture was clearly made at an earlier date, however, and it is recorded that at the coronation of Anne Boleyn plate was shown in Westminster Hall on a cupboard of ten stages. Plate 126 shows a court cupboard half-octagonal in plan, the top shelf supported by figures of exotic animals while the lower one has the more usual bulbous supports. Most court cupboards are, however, rectangular in plan and a drawer is normally to be found in the frieze. By about 1610 supports begin to adopt a simpler baluster form and the bulbs protruding from the supports of earlier examples are no longer used. This piece of furniture was soon to go into a rapid decline in popularity, few being produced, except in country areas, after 1660.

Up to the end of the sixteenth century valuables had usually been kept in small leather-covered chests or coffers in England. A few instances of cabinets provided with drawers are, however, recorded in sixteenth-century inventories of the royal household and leading families of the nobility. These must have been small and intended to stand on another piece of furniture or a stand made especially for the purpose. Most of these cabinets were no doubt foreign and larger pieces of English manufacture did not become common until the Restoration. From this period they are usually provided with matching stands. The doors that cover the drawers and the drawer fronts themselves are often decorated with marquetry work or finished in lacquer. Secret drawers and compartments are often provided for valuables, a necessary precaution in an age before the establishment of efficient methods of policing when, following the Civil War, disbanded soldiers not infrequently took to a life of crime. Some cabinets were provided with drawers in the stand, thus increasing the storage capacity. The example shown in plate 127 is not untypical of this type and the multiplicity of small drawers in the top half is usual in this type of furniture. Some cabinets of this period have domed cornices provided with stands for the display of porcelain which was being imported in increasing quantities in East India Company vessels. This habit of displaying porce-

125 *above* Court cupboard, oak, *c*.1600, with canted centre cupboard on the top tier. The centre and top friezes have drawers in them and the bottom frieze has carved arcading. (Mallett)

126 *left* Court cupboard of half octagonal shape, oak, *c*.1600. The lower supporters are of the conventional bulb type while those at the top follow continental influence and take the form of mythological winged beasts. The lowest frieze is carved with flutes, the other two being decorated with carved arabesques. (Mallett)

lain on the tops of cabinets had been introduced from Holland by Queen Mary II.

Because of their valuable contents, cabinets had a considerable degree of attention paid to their decoration and were often produced in forms that displayed the latest taste effectively. Plate 128, for instance, shows a fine cabinet japanned in red of *c.* 1730. Most late seventeenth-century lacquer cabinets of imported origin or decorated with imported lacquer panels were rectangular. This rather later japanned cabinet displays a classical Baroque broken pediment and classical urn finials. The lower portion, has a secretaire drawer for writing materials, and the cabinet is supported on a giltwood stand.

Articles contained in these enclosed cabinets could not be admired without being removed, so from the early eighteenth century display cabinets with glass panels in the door were produced, mainly for the display of oriental porcelain. These cabinets are often very architectural in form and, apart from the spacing of the shelves and their depth, are not easy to distinguish from bookcases of the same period. Many are of the break-front variety, with two recessed wings (plate 129). From the 1750s the glazing bars sometimes resemble a simplified Gothic form with lancets. Other cabinets were made with outlines in Gothic or Chinese form from *c.* 1750, and designs for such cabinets are to be found in the works of Thomas Chippendale and Ince and Mayhew. A fine example of a cabinet in the Chinese taste is illustrated in plate 130, which resembles to a marked degree plate CXXXVI of the third edition of the *Director* (1762). The pagoda roofs, geometric tracery and Rococo scroll work are very typical of the more ornate examples of this 'Chinese Chippendale' style. Such a style must have been thought most appropriate to the display of Chinese porcelain. Of approximately the same date is the cabinet in plate 131. This is a corner display cabinet in mahogany, the only carved enrichment being in the cornice and the border to the lower section of the panelled door. Numerous narrow corner cabinets and cupboards were produced in the eighteenth century. Some were provided with a stand, while others were set on a cupboard base. Plate 131 does not exactly conform to the usual practice, as it is not made in two parts.

By the last decade of the eighteenth century the architectural form of book and display cases, which had prevailed for fifty years, was superseded by a greater variety in design. Plate 132 illustrates a fine satinwood cabinet of this period. It is both lower and smaller than most earlier cabinets, and features not untypical of furniture of this period are the semi-circular recess beneath the drawer in the frieze and the brass

127 *left* Cabinet, walnut, *c.*1690, with fall front to top section providing a writing surface. The doors are decorated with feathered bandings and the quality of the piece is emphasized by the veneering of the insides of the doors. (Hotspur)

128 *below* Cabinet, japanned, *c.* 1730 with broken pediment and vase-shaped finials. The lower drawers and pigeon holes have a separate door. The cabinet has a contemporary gilt stand. (Mallett)

trellis decorating the top. Glazed display cabinets with architectural pretensions continued to be made in the Victorian period, with rosewood or walnut as alternatives to mahogany, though the glazed doors and the panels of the cupboards beneath are likely to be rounded at the top to conform with Victorian taste. Another characteristic Victorian piece of display furniture was the what-not. This consisted of a number of open shelves supported by turned supports at the corners and designed to display small decorative objects. Some were designed with shaped triangular shelves to stand in a corner. Walnut was normally used and marquetry work was a common feature. Although it is a typically Victorian piece, the what-not originated in the Regency period, examples dating from the early nineteenth century being more often in rosewood and having less shaping than Victorian pieces.

A number of attractive cabinets were produced in the 1860s, when there was a revival of interest in eighteenth-century styles, both French and English. Plate 133 shows a fine satinwood cabinet of c. 1870 enriched with floral marquetry and brass trellis and mounts. The centre panel with its urn and classical drapes suggests inspiration from the Adam period, though the swags of flowers conform more to Victorian than to eighteenth-century taste. The revived interest in eighteenth-century furniture dates from the late 1860s, an early example being a cabinet in the Adam style displayed at the Paris International Exhibition of 1867 by the London cabinet-makers Wright & Mansfield.

BOOKCASES

Domestic bookcases are not known before the Restoration. Private libraries certainly existed before this date, though they were small by eighteenth-century and later standards and books must have been stored in fitted cupboards or shelves. Public libraries such as those at Merton College, Oxford, the Bodleian Library and the Kedderminster Library at Langley Church in Buckinghamshire give some clue to the layout of libraries in this period.

One of the earliest domestic bookcases must have been that produced by Simpson the joiner in 1666 for Samuel Pepys, whose books were 'growing numerous and lying one upon another on [my] chairs'. In all Pepys had twelve similar cases made and these are now at Magdalene College, Cambridge, with his collection of books. Two similar cases were made for Dryham Park in Gloucestershire; one of these is now to be seen in the Victoria and Albert Museum (plate 134). The cases are architectural in form and apart from the glazing of the base section conform closely to the pat-

129 *above left* Display cabinet,
mahogany, *c.*1765, of break front
type. The cornice is decorated with
carved dentil moulding and
surmounted by a scrolled pediment.
The astragals (glazing bars) are
suggestive of Gothic form.
(Mallett)

130 *left* Display cabinet,
mahogany with gilt enrichment,
*c.*1760, in the Chinese taste with
pagoda roofs, and astragals in the
wing sections of geometrical fret
pattern. (Mallett)

131 *above* Corner cupboard
mahogany, *c.*1760, both upper and
lower sections covered by one door.
Cornice enriched with carved scroll
decoration. (Harris)

132 *left* Display cabinet, satinwood with bandings of other woods, *c.*1790. The top of the cabinet is decorated with a brass gallery while brass trellis work is used on the fronts of the lower cupboard doors. (Mallett)

133 *below* Cabinet, satinwood with marquetry in various woods and applied metal mounts and gallery, *c.*1870. This is an example of the revival in interest in the styles and techniques of the eighteenth century. (Victoria & Albert Museum)

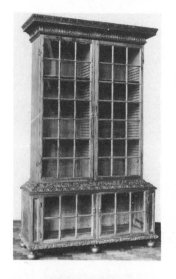

134 *above left* Bookcase, oak, *c*.1670, from Dyrham Park in Gloucestershire, and similar in style to ones made for Samuel Pepys from 1666. (Victoria & Albert Museum)

135 *above* Bureau bookcase, burr walnut and banded, *c*.1710, with shaped cornice enriched with three finials. The doors to the bookcase are faced with mirror glass. (Mallett)

136 *left* Bookcase, mahogany, *c*.1770, with geometrical astragals, frieze carved with scroll work and quatrefoils and scrolled broken pediment above the cornice. (Mallett)

tern adopted subsequently for this type of furniture. By the reign of
Queen Anne bookcases were quite frequently incorporated as an upper
stage to a bureau (plate 135). In this form the bookcase section is often
fitted with wooden doors or mirror plates and the books are not exposed
to view. The double-gabled serpentine top in the example illustrated in
plate 135 is frequently found in larger case furniture of this period.

The extensive fitting out of libraries in Georgian country houses as pres-
tige rooms does not appear to have taken place on any scale before *c.* 1730,
but from this date onwards libraries become a normal feature of domestic
interiors. Bookcases are invariably architectural in form. Many examples
of the period 1730–60 are surmounted by a broken pediment; although
this device was used after 1760, the broken scroll pediment as shown in
plate 136 was more common after this date. Larger bookcases had the
break-front arrangement (plate 137), as did larger display cabinets and
wardrobes. Shelves for books usually occupied only the top half of the
bookcase, the lower section being provided with drawers or cupboards
for storage. A number of late eighteenth-century bookcases have a secretaire drawer. The front of what appears at first sight to be a deep top
drawer falls in an arc to provide a writing surface and to reveal a succession of small drawers or pigeon holes designed for writing materials and
correspondence (plate 137). The Gothic and Chinese tastes, which influenced much furniture design in the mid-eighteenth century, had little
effect on bookcases as the shaping essential to these styles would have
restricted their storage capacity. By the 1780s a number of smaller types of
bookcase were being developed, so that limited quantities of books
needed for immediate reading and consultation could be kept in rooms
other than the library. These included small, low, open bookshelves, often
decorated with a brass trellis in Regency examples, and described in contemporary literature as 'moving libraries'. These could not only be placed
against walls but could be kept close to chairs to satisfy immediate reading
needs. Plate 138 shows a combined table and bookshelves (known as a
Bonheur du jour) in the Adam taste. The marquetry of paterae on the frame
above the legs and swags draped between is typical of the decoration used
in the 1770s and 1780s. The tapering square-section legs which terminate
in spade feet are a very characteristic late eighteenth-century type.

During the Regency period dwarf bookcases were produced, these
being much lower in height. George Smith declared in his *Household
Furniture* (1808) that this was so that the walls could be left free for displaying pictures. These bookcases, often produced in pairs, are frequently a
subject for treatment in the 'archaeological' style associated with Thomas

137 *left* Secretaire bookcase, mahogany, *c.*1780, of break front type. A relatively plain piece of furniture which relies upon its proportion, the quality of the veneers and its workmanship for effect. (Mallett)

138 *below left* Writing table with bookshelves above (Bonheur du Jour), harewood with satinwood banding, marquetry and ormolu mounts, *c.*1770. (Mallett)

139 *below right* Bookcase, rosewood with metal mounts in the Egyptian taste, *c.*1810. (Mallett)

140 *top right* Revolving bookcase, rosewood, *c.*1820. (Harris)

141 *far right* Bookcase, oak, *c.* 1860 in two sections with carved enrichment including a medallion of Shakespeare in the cornice frieze. (Victoria & Albert Museum)

Hope. The feet of bookcases are often shaped in the form of animal paws and their main vertical members are ornamented with lion or chimera masks. A similar treatment is accorded to the bookcase in plate 139. Here the cast brass heads are Egyptian, and the star motifs on the blocks beneath the feet are also frequently found in furniture in this style. The full extent of the civilization of Ancient Egypt was a new discovery in the Regency period, and it excited very considerable interest. The invasion of Egypt by Napoleon's forces in 1797 and the subsequent defeat of the French fleet at the Battle of the Nile and the occupation of Egypt by British soldiers brought the country into public view. With Napoleon's army travelled Baron Vivant Denon, whose book *Voyages dans la Basse et Haute Égypte* (1802) provided the visual evidence of this civilization for the European reader. The Egyptian taste in furniture continued until the late 1820s.

The Regency admiration for round and drum tables has already been noted (see pp. 57, 60). This interest is also to be seen in the revolving bookcases that enjoyed a brief popularity in this period. Designs and examples dating from the first decade of the nineteenth century are known but the example shown in plate 140 is probably about twenty years later, as it has a pronounced 'knee' carved with acanthus at the top of the claw legs, a feature still to be found in early Victorian tables on similar supports. An interesting feature is the use of false book fronts, made necessary by the circular shape.

Victorian bookcases, although departing little from their Georgian counterparts in outline, have much more carved detail and ornamentation. In the Victorian period the Gothic style was considered most suitable for libraries, and in an attempt to come nearer to the authentic Gothic taste oak began to be favoured. Plate 141 shows a Victorian bookcase of *c.* 1860, though in this case the carved decoration with the central medallion of Shakespeare appears to owe more to early Renaissance than to Gothic influence. When bookcases of the early Victorian period are produced in the Grecian style, a continuation of the Regency styling, the outline tends to be disfigured by the application of clumsy, heavily carved, cornice brackets.

DESKS AND BUREAUX

Portable writing desks have a long history, extending back in England as far as the Middle Ages. A fine example fitted with drawers and finished in gilt and painted leather can be seen in the Victoria and Albert Museum and can be confidently dated to *c.* 1525, but most surviving examples from the sixteenth and early seventeenth centuries are much plainer, consisting

142 *above* Portable desk, walnut, *c*.1720, fitted with
drawers and pigeon holes and with a lower drawer
below the desk flap of which the front is in bombé
form. (Mallett)

143 *below* Secretaire, walnut, *c*.1700, with fall flap.
Two drawers are contained in the desk with a
further one in the stand. (Hotspur)

144 *left* Bureau, oak,
c.1700, with sloping fall
front on ball feet.
(Hotspur)

145 *below* Kneehole
writing table, mahogany,
c.1750, with central
cupboard in the kneehole.
(Mallett)

of a carved oak box with a sloping surface at the top on which a book or papers can be laid for reading. Such pieces are frequently referred to as 'Bible boxes', but the provision of compartments in the interior for storing writing materials indicates their true function. Occasionally, especially c. 1600, desks were elaborately inlaid and at least one example exists with architectural inlay of the 'Nonsuch' pattern (see pp. 65–7). Portable desks continued to be made in the late seventeenth and eighteenth centuries, though the popularity of such pieces declined with the introduction of the bureau. Plate 142 shows an example of a portable desk of c. 1720, a period when such desks had matching stands, the legs being of cabriole form. Later examples exist, but are in most cases designed solely for travelling. The demand was still sufficient at the end of the eighteenth century for Thomas Shearer to include a design in the *Cabinet Maker's London Book of Prices* (1788).

The bureau as we understand it, consisting of a chest of drawers surmounted by a desk with a sloping fall front, was not developed until c. 1700, but rectangular writing cabinets on stands with a fall front, usually referred to in contemporary documents as 'scriptors', appear from late in the reign of Charles II, while these writing cabinets on a stand were the usual form by the 1690s. These pieces of furniture developed at a period when the British public had for the first time in its history an efficient official national postal system. The example illustrated in plate 143 shows many of the characteristics of the bureau, such as the pull-out lopers on which the sloping front rests when lowered to provide a flat writing surface. It is also clear that it is descended from the portable desk. This type of escritoire continued to be made in the eighteenth century as a lady's writing desk.

The bureau is the form that has remained popular to this day was developed in about 1700. Plate 144 shows an example from the early eighteenth century, which is supported on ball feet. The use of oak for this piece suggests that it may be the work of a small country cabinet-maker. More fashionable bureaux of this period would have been veneered in walnut. Contemporary with the development of the bureau is that of the bureau cabinet and a few examples exist of tallboys fitted with a secretaire in either the top drawer of the lower section or the bottom drawer of the upper section. A number of bureau cabinets of the early eighteenth century are elaborately finished in japan work. Bureau bookcases were also in production by the early Georgian period. Examples from c. 1750 dispense with the sloping front to the bureau and instead adopt a deep secretaire drawer that lets down on a quadrant.

146 *above* Pedestal writing table, mahogany, late eighteenth century with tooled leather top. (Mallett)

147 *left* Cylinder writing desk, satinwood with banding and stringing, *c.* 1795. (Mallett)

148 *left* Davenport, mahogany, *c.*1800, with brass gallery, four drawers in the side and candle slide. (Harris)

149 *left* Desk, mahogany, *c.*1840, with fall front to top section and turned colonettes at the front corners. (Victoria & Albert Museum)

Some bureaux were provided with a recessed centre section, and this feature was also widely adopted for the knee-hole desk or writing table (plate 145). This type of desk with drawers in the pillars and a recessed centre cupboard was produced in walnut from *c.* 1700 and mahogany versions began to appear about thirty years later. A larger form of writing table, frequently referred to as a 'partner's desk', was made throughout the eighteenth century and into the nineteenth (plate 146). Such tables were suitable for business premises or libraries, though special library tables were also produced following this form. The finer mid- and late eighteenth-century examples are much more elaborately decorated with carving, lion masks being particularly favoured before *c.* 1770, and elaborate marquetry in the Adam taste appearing on later examples.

A development in bureaux and secretaires in the last two decades of the eighteenth century was the roll-top or cylinder type. Both Sheraton and Hepplewhite published designs for secretaires with these tambour fronts. By this period the provision of drawers down to ground level was less favoured and many secretaires had the tapering square-section legs favoured by Hepplewhite, though a superstructure of small drawers and bookshelves might be provided (plate 147). Some writing tables of this period also had a structure of small drawers on the top forming a horseshoe at the back and on two sides. Such tables are known as 'Carlton House tables', though there is no evidence to connect their origin with the Prince of Wales, whose London home was Carlton House, except that a table in this form at present in Buckingham Palace is believed to have come from Carlton House.

A new type of desk introduced in the Regency period and destined to find considerable favour in the early Victorian age was the davenport. It consisted of a narrow case of drawers with a sloping writing surface, the drawers acting as receptacles for writing materials. The example illustrated in plate 148 has, in addition to the drawers in the side, a slide at the top, which is intended to provide a platform for a candlestick. The name of this piece of furniture appears to have been derived from a Captain Davenport, for whom the cabinet-makers Gillows of Lancaster produced a desk of this type. J. C. Loudon mentions their use in drawing rooms and declares them to be 'very useful articles for industrious young ladies'. Victorian examples are usually in walnut enriched with carved decoration and marquetry. The desk top is usually extended forward from the pedestal containing the drawers and is held by two supports, often of a curvilinear shape, extending to the plinth. One example described as a davenport and illustrated in *The Cabinet-Makers Assistant* (1853) has no drawers beneath the sloping writing surface, which is supported on four carved pillars. The top of the desk is surmounted by carved fret at the back.

A secretaire of the conventional form but dating from the Victorian era is illustrated in plate 149. The bulbous wooden knobs, wooden keyhole escutcheons and knob-turned supports ending in short turned feet are typical features of case furniture of the early Victorian period. The fine figure of the mahogany veneers on this piece should be noted. No cock bead is used on the drawers but a half-round moulding has been applied to the framing between the drawers. The top drawer is shaped both in elevation and plan, while the fall front is surrounded by a heavy bolection moulding.

SIDEBOARDS

Before *c.* 1770 the sideboard was not in any sense an item for storage. As its name implies it was a 'board', that is a table, which stood at the side of the dining room so that food could be placed on it before it was served. Because it had to accept hot dishes it was usually fitted with a marble top. Such tables closely followed the design of side tables intended mainly for ornamental purposes in drawing rooms. No attempt was made to provide drawers in the table for napery, cutlery and so on, so this must have been brought into the room for each meal. This rather inconvenient arrangement began to be modified in *c.* 1770.

It is in the drawings of Robert Adam that we find for the first time designs not only for sideboard tables but also for pedestals surmounted by urns and for wine coolers *en suite* with the table. The pedestals which stood on either side of the table provided general storage space, acted as a cellaret for storing wine bottles or were used as a cupboard in which plates could be warmed, or glasses washed in a lead-lined cistern. The urns surmounting them were usually knife boxes in which cutlery could be kept, though in some cases they were lined with lead and used as water cisterns. Sideboard tables with pedestals and urns are found in a number of houses for which Adam was commissioned to design interiors, such as Kenwood and Osterley in Middlesex, Saltram in Devonshire and Harewood and Newby in Yorkshire. Adam is known to have designed the first three and the drawing for the Kenwood sideboard was published by the Adam brothers in their *Works in Architecture* (1773). Chippendale and Haig were responsible for the Harewood sideboard suite, which was probably designed by Thomas Chippendale, while the Newby example is attributed to Thomas Chippendale Jr. A pair of pedestals with urns in the

150 *left* Pedestals, mahogany, carved and cross-banded, *c*.1775. (Harris)

151 *right* Sideboard, mahogany with satinwood banding and stringing, *c*.1790, on square-section tapering legs terminating in spade feet. (Hotspur)

152 *left* Sideboard made by William Morris & Co. painted with figures of women and birds by E. Burne-Jones, June 1860. (Victoria & Albert Museum)

153 *left* Sideboard, ebonized wood, with inset panels of embossed Japanese leather paper. Designed by E. W. Godwin and made by William Watt, 1867. (Victoria & Albert Museum)

Adam tradition is shown in plate 150.

In his *Cabinet-Maker's and Upholsterer's Guide* (1788) George Hepplewhite illustrates sideboard tables, pedestals and vases in the Adam taste, but he also includes a sideboard table incorporating drawers beneath the frieze and a cupboard at each end. This type of sideboard was already in production by this date, for in 1779 Gillows had supplied one of a similar construction. The great advantage of the new combined type of sideboard was that it took up much less room than the Adam version and was therefore suited to the smaller rooms of middle-class homes and town houses. A wine cooler could be placed under the centre part of the sideboard or wine stored in one of the side cupboards, which would be lined with lead for the purpose. This type of sideboard was also illustrated by Shearer and Sheraton in their designs. As with contemporary chests of drawers, sideboards can be serpentine, bow-fronted or straight-fronted. The example shown in plate 151 is not untypical of this type, which often show fine figure in the veneer and attractive banding.

Sheraton's designs for sideboards show a brass gallery at the back. This feature was incorporated in the Adam sideboard for Kenwood but is a rare feature before the 1790s, though it was common during the two decades that followed. Regency sideboards from *c.* 1805 tend to become monumental and use lion monopodia as supports under the influence of Thomas Hope. The Regency also tended to favour a return to pedestals, which acted as supports for the detachable sideboard table top. Although separate knife boxes were provided with some Regency sideboards the urn type used by Robert Adam did not find favour.

Victorian sideboards carry on the tradition of the Regency with regard to size. The pedestal form was still popular in the early Victorian period, though now the table top was attached. J. C. Loudon illustrates two sideboard tables with brass trellis at the back, sarcophagus wine coolers and carved front supports (in one design lion monopodia), which he wrongly declares to be 'in the style of Louis XIV'. The designs in *The Cabinet-Maker's Assistant* (1853) show a similar trend, being either of the pedestal type, or 'slab sideboards' consisting of a marble-topped sideboard table with a carved backboard. A number of sideboards have mirror backs and are decorated with carved ornamentation. Sideboards appear to have been regarded as pieces of furniture of prime importance by the Victorians and on the more ornate examples carved ornament was lavished with utter disregard to function. One of the most ornate examples is the Chevy Chase sideboard commissioned for the Duke of Northumberland, which is 10ft high, 12ft wide and 4½ft deep. The carving was executed by Gerrard Robinson, who worked continuously on it from 1855 to 1890, the year of his death.

In utter contrast to the heaviness and ornateness of most Victorian sideboards is the example illustrated in plate 152, which was produced by William Morris & Co in June 1860. Apart from the range of simple craftsman-made furniture produced at competitive prices for a wide market, such as the Sussex chair (see plate 55), Morris produced a number of individual commissions for wealthy patrons (state furniture). With these Morris had the medieval ideals of craftsmanship in mind; the construction was sound but simple and the pieces were decorated with painted scenes by noted artists, mainly members of the Pre-Raphaelite Brotherhood. The sideboard illustrated was painted by E. Burne-Jones. By using painted decoration Morris was working in a medieval tradition, for much furniture in the Middle Ages was painted. William Burgess, an architect who also designed furniture, was another Victorian medievalist who favoured the use of furniture decorated with painted scenes. Burgess was designing for individual commissions and not for commercial production. The stand of designers like Burgess and Morris against the extravagant and meaningless ornament in much Victorian design was to have considerable effect not only in Britain, for it was also to inspire progressive furniture designers of the twentieth century such as Gerrit Rietveld in Holland and Marcel Breuer and Walter Gropius in Germany.

Another pioneer in the development of modern design was the architect E. W. Godwin. He was particularly influenced by the art of Japan, which was at that period being fully revealed in the West for the first time following the opening up of the country to international trade. The clean lines and successful relationship of solid and void in the sideboard illustrated in plate 153 give this piece a strikingly modern appearance, yet it was made in 1867. Godwin used ebonized wood, which frames the panels of Japanese leather paper. The elegant yet simple metal fittings are of silver to provide contrast. E. W. Godwin designed furniture for a number of manufacturers, including William Watt (the makers of the sideboard), Collinson and Lock and Gillows. It must be emphasized however that the work of Morris and Godwin illustrated here was in marked contrast to much furniture produced commercially at the time. This may, however, do something to dispel the idea that there was a Victorian style, for the history of English furniture in the period from the mid-1830s to the end of the century is complex. The Victorians borrowed from many sources and adapted many past styles that cannot be described fully in the space available.

4 Beds and Bedroom Furniture

THE BED has a long history, because, like the chest, table and chair, it satisfies one of the most fundamental of man's furnishing needs. The bed of the Middle Ages consisted of little more than a wooden frame, the mattress being supported on a mesh of ropes fixed to the frame. A canopy or tester was suspended from the ceiling, though by late in the fifteenth century posts were being used to support it in some cases. Surrounding the bed were curtains, which were very necessary to keep out draughts. The woodwork of the bed was of little value compared with the hangings, which in the houses of the great landowners and merchants were of rich imported cloth.

By the sixteenth century a panelled headboard was attached to the bed frame and a wooden canopy extended from the top of this to the front posts. In the late sixteenth century considerable care was lavished upon the posts, headboard and cornice of the beds, which were richly carved and inlaid (plate 154). Until well into the eighteenth century the bedroom was much more public than it is today. Important visitors might be received there, and the births of children were spectacles attended by numerous relatives and other interested persons. The bed had therefore as much attention lavished on its decoration and hangings as important pieces of furniture in the main reception rooms. The Great Bed of Ware in the Victoria and Albert Museum has a height of 8ft 9in and in length and width is 10ft 8in. If we are to believe Paul Hentzner, a German visitor to England in 1598, this bed was not unique in size, though few surviving examples

154 *right* Bed, oak with inlay on the frieze and headboard, *c*.1600. The bulbous front supports end in Corinthian capitals and the backboard is panelled and arcaded. (Mallett)

155 *left* Bed, mahogany, *c*.1740, with fluted bedposts with Corinthian capitals. The frieze is decorated with Vitruvian scroll and dentil mouldings and the cornice is surmounted by a cartouche. (Victoria & Albert Museum)

156 *left* Bed, mahogany, *c.*1770, the cornice frieze is carved with a border of round paterae between flutes. (Harris)

157 *below* Night tables, mahogany with box stringing, *c.*1790. These are usually produced in pairs to stand one on either side of the bed. (Harris)

are as large. Because of the costliness of the bed hangings and the importance of this piece of furniture beds are frequently described in detail in wills and inventories, whereas other pieces of furniture feature only briefly.

Although the woodwork of beds was less ornate in the seventeenth century the hangings became even more magnificent. Beds increased in height to take advantage of the full height of the room and by 1690 were decorated at the top with elaborate cutwork or plumes of ostrich feathers. The state bed of William III, for instance, is 17ft to the top of the ostrich plumes, while the Melville Bed at the Victoria and Albert Museum is 15ft 2in. The state beds of country houses in the eighteenth century kept up the tradition of magnificence.

Although most surviving examples do not approach in elegance the state beds of large houses, they follow a similar pattern. The bed in plate 155 (of about 1740) is of distinctly architectural appearance in the tradition of William Kent. The cornice is supported by Corinthian columns, while the lower part of the cornice is decorated with carved Vitruvian scroll moulding. The bed is surmounted by a carved cartouche framed by scrolls. Plate 156 shows a bed of thirty years later with elegant fluted bedposts supporting a cornice decorated with medallions and flutes in the Adam taste. In both plates 155 and 156 the beds lack the full set of hangings, which would have been designed to fit into the general decorative scheme of the room and would have obscured some of the woodwork of the bed.

In the two decades that followed 1750 bedrooms were often decorated in the Chinese taste, one of the most lavish examples being at Claydon in Buckinghamshire. Beds and other pieces of furniture were designed to conform with this taste and one of the finest examples of a bed in this 'Chinese Chippendale' style is one from Badminton House in Gloucestershire, which is now in the Victoria and Albert Museum. For many years this bed was attributed to Thomas Chippendale on stylistic grounds, but it is now recognized as a product of William Linnell's workshop, the design being that of his son John Linnell.

An alternative to the 'four poster' was the tent or field bed. This was a single bed fitted with four posts which carried a light arched framework on which the curtains were draped. These beds were suited to cottages and smaller houses. Horace Walpole mentions their use as early as 1752 and eighty years later J. C. Loudon could declare that 'tent beds are in universal use and scarcely require description'. An alternative type of bed favoured in the early nineteenth century was the French bed. This had

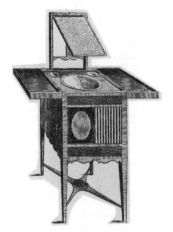

158 *above* Basin stands, designs by Thomas Shearer
from the *Cabinet-Maker's London Book of Prices* (1788),
plate 11. These were almost invariably produced
from mahogany. The two cups were for soap.

curtains either draped from a pole fixed to the wall above the bed or hung
from a domed tester.

By the 1830s, when Loudon was writing, a considerable change was
taking place in bed construction. Cast iron was beginning to replace wood
as a construction material. Although Loudon described a number of beds
made of wood he also declared of wooden bedsteads with sacking bottoms
that 'these materials are apt to harbour vermin, they have lately been
manufactured entirely of wrought iron; the place of the sacking or canvas
bottom being supplied by interwoven thin iron hooping'. The use of
metal bedsteads gradually gained ground, with Birmingham becoming a
major centre of production, and by the 1870s brass and iron beds had
become almost universal. Papier mâché was also used for bed production
and a half-tester bed in the Victoria and Albert Museum has panels of this
material with posts of japanned iron. The nineteenth century particularly
favoured convertible beds that folded up into cupboards (press beds) or
couches that extended to form beds, though press beds have a much longer
history, reaching back to at least the seventeenth century.

A further essential of the bedroom was a receptacle for a chamber pot. Until the middle of the eighteenth century this took the form of a box-like container with a rising lid known as a 'close stool'. From *c.* 1750, however, night tables or pot cupboards took over this function, usually being produced in pairs. The example shown in plate 157 is typical of this piece of furniture and the basic simplicity of shaping, the fine figure of the mahogany and the lines of stringing would suggest a date *c.* 1790.

Washstands were also to be found in the bedroom, though no special piece of furniture for this purpose appears to have been produced until the middle of the eighteenth century. Such stands, which were usually of mahogany, had provision for a basin and a soap container. Examples of the Chippendale period are usually little more than open-work basin stands but most later washstands were designed with folding lids to cover the basin and resembled a small cabinet in appearance (plate 158). Mirrors were incorporated in some washstands. In the Victorian period washstands were much larger and usually incorporated a marble top.

Dressing tables are known from the Restoration period but most pieces of this nature consisted merely of a small table with drawers beneath, three being the usual number. By *c.* 1725 an alternative form resembling a kneehole desk was also being produced. The top drawer contained a mirror designed to fold down flat when not in use and a number of compartments for toilet requisites. Some chests of drawers were produced with a fitted top drawer similar in function. Plate 159 shows a dressing table of *c.* 1765 in the 'Gothick' style of the period. This had been popularized by Horace Walpole's advocacy of the style and the publicity given to his 'Gothick' house, Strawberry Hill, at Twickenham in Middlesex. In this example the two top flaps of the dressing table folded back to reveal the wells and compartments and also to provide an additional surface area. A cabinet is also incorporated at the back, but this is not a common feature.

Separate toilet mirrors, often mounted on a base incorporating drawers for toilet necessities, were also produced from the late seventeenth century in considerable numbers. By the late eighteenth century drawer fronts were either bow, serpentine or straight to suit the taste of the buyer and often a shield-shaped mirror was adopted to fit in with the popularity of the type of chair-back associated with the name of George Hepplewhite.

For chests of drawers and wardrobes see pp. 69–71 and 81–84.

Cradles, though not specifically bedroom furniture, are worth a brief mention at this point. Of those that survive the majority are of seventeenth-century date. These are of sturdy frame and panel con-

159 *left* Dressing table, mahogany, *c.*1765, with cabinet at the back. This piece shows a pierced geometrical frieze in the Chinese taste, but the scroll mouldings on the cabinet doors are in ogee Gothic form terminating in pagoda roofs. This mixture of motifs from different tastes in the furniture of this period is not unusual. (Harris)

160 *below* Cradle, oak *c.*1700. The fielded panels (Chamfered edges with flat centre) used on this piece would suggest a late date but similar cradles on rockers were produced from the beginning of the seventeenth century. (Geffrye Museum)

struction and have a hood over the head which is hinged at one side to keep draughts off the child. The cradles have rockers and posts at the front and head, presumably to facilitate the process of rocking (plate 160). This type of cradle continued to be made well into the eighteenth century. We have drawings of later types by Thomas Sheraton, George Smith and J. C. Loudon, among others, but few surviving examples. These not only lacked the solid construction of earlier examples but by their very nature were objects with a limited usefulness and thus had a high mortality rate.

5 Other Items of Furniture

MIRRORS

The production of looking glasses in England may not have begun in commercial quantities until the Restoration. A petition to Parliament in 1621 from Sir Robert Mansell, who held the patents for the production of Venetian glass, claimed that he had produced looking glasses, but there are no surviving examples of this period. In 1664, however, the Worshipful Company of Glass-sellers and Looking-glass Makers was set up and a few years later George Villiers, 2nd Duke of Buckingham, was controlling a glass works at Vauxhall where looking glasses were produced. John Evelyn, the diarist, visited the works in 1676 and declared the looking glasses to be 'larger and better than any that come from Venice', though it is clear from existing English mirrors of this period that the plates produced were little more than 3ft square, and that larger and finer plates were still imported. Such imported glass could be expensive: three mirrors supplied to the Royal Household by John Gumley and James Moore in 1714 and 1715 cost £120, £156 and £149 respectively.

Mirror frames faithfully reflect the tastes prevalent in interior decoration and furnishing. The square plates of the Restoration period are frequently mounted in elaborately carved frames displaying festoons of flowers, foliage and fruit, heads of cherubs (*putti*) and birds in the tradition associated with Grinling Gibbons and the English Baroque. Frames of carved softwood are often silvered or gilt (plate 161). Alternative finishes used in this period include frames of stump work (raised needlework), tortoiseshell, parquetry work in laburnum or olive, Anglo-Dutch floral marquetry and lacquer. Imported lacquer often came into the country in the form of sixfold screens, which were then cut up and used as veneers on cabinets and other furniture. Offcuts might be used on a mirror frame in rather bizarre combinations. In their *Treatise of Japanning and Varnishing*

161 *above* Mirror in carved and silvered frame *c.*1670 with carving of amorini (cupids) and foliage in the taste of Grinling Gibbons. (Spink)

162 *above* Mirror in gilt frame decorated with panels and cresting of *verre eglomisé*, displaying arabesques, swags of flowers and a morini, *c.* 1695. (Mallett)

163 *below* Mirror in walnut frame with carved and gilt enrichment, *c.*1740. The top of the frame incorporates a broken scroll pediment with a central cartouche. (Mallett)

164 *below* Mirror, carved and gilt frame, *c.*1755, in the Chinese taste with a frame of scrolled foliage and surmounted by a pagoda. (Mallett)

165 *above left* Mirror, carved and gilt frame, *c.* 1775, in the neo-classical taste. Swags of husks are draped from an urn surmounting the frame. Oval glasses are characteristic of this period. (Mallett)

166 *above* Mirror in carved and gilt frame *c.*1815. Circular convex mirrors were popular during the Regency and the eagle a favourite subject for the cresting. (Harris)

167 *below left* One of a pair of girandoles, carved and gilt, *c.* 1760, of asymmetrical form carrying two candle arms. (Hotspur)

(1685) Stalker and Parker record 'angling for Dolphins in a Wood, or pursuing the Stag, and chasing the Boar in the middle of the Ocean'. During the reign of Charles II mirrors were produced *en suite* with the table above which they were to hang, together with a pair of floor-standing candlestands.

Mirror frames of the late seventeenth century are often rectangular and have a cresting fixed above them (plate 161). By *c.* 1690, however, mirrors had commonly become elongated to fit the height of the rooms in the houses then being built. They usually consisted of more than one plate, the joins being covered by decorative bead. The head of the top plate was semi-circular. Frames and cresting are often of *verre eglomisé* (painted on the underside of the glass and backed with metal foil) (plate 162). though gilt and carved frames were still fashionable.

Mirrors in walnut frames became popular in the early Georgian period, with carved gilt detail to afford a contrast. This made a less expensive frame than the carved gilt ones that were still produced for more opulent patrons. Both types began to take on a more architectural form in *c.* 1730. The example shown in plate 163 shows the popular scrolled pediment used by numerous makers at this period. Shell motifs were also prominently featured.

The Rococo taste popular from *c.* 1750 provided an ideal form for the mirror frame carver. The intricate pattern of C and S scrolls gave scope for infinite variety and although most English mirror frames are symmetrical, the asymmetrical form more popular on the Continent could also be adopted. The Chinese taste particularly appealed to mirror-frame carvers and pagodas, bells, icicles, long-necked birds and mandarins are all to be found. Plate 164 shows a mirror frame mildly Chinese in taste with a pagoda featured at the top, though the remainder consists of relatively tame sinuous scrolls of foliage. The mirror frame is symmetrical and a charming feature is the use of twin dogs facing one another carved in the side frames.

One of the most lavish exponents of Rococo carving was Thomas Johnson, whose designs for mirror frames best exemplify this phase, though Mathias Lock, Thomas Chippendale and Ince and Mayhew also provide numerous alternative designs.

The method of casting glass plates introduced into France *c.* 1670 was not used in England until 1776 and large plates still had to be imported. Chippendale was involved in the importation of French glass. Large plates were thus still expensive, and in June 1778, when Chippendale and Haig forwarded a quotation to Sir William Knatchbull at Mersham-le-Hatch in Kent for mirrors, the prices quoted for the plates were from £155 to £180 each, while the frames were only £28 to £36.

Adam's neo-classical revolution was soon reflected in mirror frames, and classical motifs such as swags of husks, anthemion, winged sphinxes and urns were introduced. Simple outlines and delicate decoration were favoured. Oval mirrors were produced (plate 165), though overmantel and pier mirrors retained a basic rectangular form. The early Regency period (c. 1800) saw the popularization of circular convex mirrors of the Empire type, though convex mirrors plates had been made in France from 1756 and had probably been imported into England soon after this date. Regency frames were often surmounted by an eagle and not infrequently had candle sconces attached to the side (plate 166). Glass painting and the use of *verre eglomisé* came back into fashion at the end of the eighteenth century and in the Regency period.

Victorian mirror frames are in the prevailing Renaissance, Gothic or Grecian styles. With a number of notable exceptions Victorian mirrors are framed in a relatively restrained manner. J. C. Loudon had attacked ornate mirrors as 'a fertile source of bad taste in articles formed for those who have abundant wealth' and advocated, especially for large plates, frames that are 'simple and architectural, seeming to belong to the construction of the room'. Although some frames were gilt, the use of oak, mahogany, walnut and other polished timbers was also favoured. Plate glass was much cheaper in Victorian times and was frequently incorporated in pieces of furniture such as sideboards, chiffoniers and wardrobes. Chiffoniers with high mirror backs are illustrated in *The Cabinet-Maker's Assistant* (1853) and a cabinet designed by the Frenchman Eugéne Prignot and made by Jackson and Graham in 1855 (now at the Victoria and Albert Museum) is decorated in similar manner with a large mirror plate.

Closely akin to mirrors are sconces (wall candleholders). These are usually of brass or silver up to the beginning of the eighteenth century, when wooden ones began to be produced, some with mirror backs to reflect the light of the candle. This type of sconce was particularly popular in the mid-eighteenth century and the French term '*girandole*' was adopted for them by the trade. Like mirror frames, they were the work of specialist carvers, Thomas Johnson being the leading designer, and like contemporary mirrors they show the full Rococo repertoire. They were often asymmetrical in form but were usually supplied in corresponding pairs. The giltwood example shown in plate 167 was no doubt the right-hand one of a pair. Carved wooden brackets were also produced from the late seventeenth century to the end of the Georgian period. These were used as

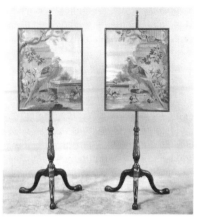

168 *above* Pole screens, mahogany, *c.* 1760, with panels of Soho tapestry. The poles on tripod bases are carved with acanthus and terminate in acorn finials. (Harris)

169 *below* Cheval screen, papier mâché, *c.* 1845, in the revived Elizabethan style with strapwork and cabochon decoration. The screen bears the impressed mark of Jennens and Bettridge of Birmingham. (Victoria & Albert Museum)

170 *below* Canterbury, rosewood with box stringing on short turned supports and with drawer underneath *c.*1810. (Harris)

supports either for pieces of porcelain (especially porcelain figures) or for clocks. A fine collection of mid-eighteenth-century brackets forms part of the Gubbay Collection which is on show at Clandon Park near Guildford in Surrey.

SCREENS

Screens can be divided into two types:

1. *Large folding screens* consisting of anything from four to twelve leaves and designed to exclude draughts from a room. These are made of various materials, including embroidery panels, leather and lacquer, the later being particularly popular from the late seventeenth century when they were brought into the country in considerable quantities.

2. *Fire screens*. The usual design for these up to the 1730s involved a framed flat panel covered in needlework set on a pair of scrolled feet. This type of screen continued to be made after the 1730s but then had a rival in the form of the pole screen. This consisted of a panel, again often of needlework, that could slide up and down a pole supported on a tripod base (plate 168). These screens were necessary to protect people sitting near the fire from the fierce heat emitted by the open basket grates then in use. This was particularly necessary in the case of women, whose cosmetics had a grease base. During the Regency and early Victorian periods pole screens with banners attached to a cross support were sometimes favoured instead of the rigid panel covered in needlework, pleated silk or painted material. Some nineteenth-century pole screens are fitted with a brass pole. Pole screens became less popular as the nineteenth century progressed and were rarely made after 1850. J. C. Loudon declared them to be less necessary because of the 'improved modes of heating used in connection with open fires, which by raising an even temperature in every part of the room, lessen the inducement for the company to collect round the fire'.

The earlier type of cheval fire screen continued to be made and is described by Thomas Chippendale in *The Director* as a 'horse' fire screen. Plate 169 shows a Victorian cheval fire screen of *c*. 1845, the frame of which has been designed in conscious imitation of the decorative taste of the period of Elizabeth I. This influence is clearly visible in the strapwork frame to the shield at the top. In complete contrast, the painted panel shows a Victorian couple in a parkland setting. The cheval fire screen retained its popularity when the pole screen fell from favour because of its usefulness in hiding empty fireplaces.

CANTERBURIES

This term is applied to low stands designed to be placed near a piano to accommodate bound volumes of music. The earliest examples appear to date from *c.* 1800 and Thomas Sheraton in his *Cabinet Dictionary* (1803) applies the term not only to a music stand but also to 'a supper tray made to stand by a table at supper, with a circular end, of three partitions cross-wise, to hold knives, forks, and plates at that end'. Plate and cutlery stands of this type exist but are not today referred to as canterburies. The name is said by Sheraton to have been applied to these pieces because the Archbishop of Canterbury first placed orders for them.

The example shown in plate 170 was made in about 1810 and has the slim, turned legs ending in brass cup castors frequently found on tables of this period. Beneath the music rack is a drawer for sheet music and a handle is pierced in the centre support of the rack—both typical features. Canterburies continued to be made in the Victorian period with increasingly elaborate shaping and carving, though their popularity was on the wane by 1850. They were occasionally produced in papier mâché in the early Victorian period. Today they find favour in furnishing schemes as magazine racks.

MUSIC STANDS

These appear to have originated in the second half of the eighteenth century and are referred to in contemporary documents as desks. The height of the centre pillar on most examples is adjustable and candleholders are not infrequently provided on either side of the stand. Examples of this type appear in the work of Ince and Mayhew and Hepplewhite. The stand shown in plate 171 is of Regency date with the main support in the form of an arrow. Although this one is of metal, the majority are of wooden construction, with a metal stem to hold the desk and provide for adjustment. One example illustrated by J. C. Loudon in his *Encyclopaedia* (1833) has the added advantage that the desk top could be folded flat so that with the support fully retracted it could be used as a small table.

DUMB WAITERS

A dumb waiter consists of a stand, often on a tripod base, usually with three revolving trays of decreasing size mounted above (plate 172). It was probably introduced early in the eighteenth century and found considerable favour. It enabled food and drink to be left conveniently near the table so that guests could help themselves during the course of the meal. It

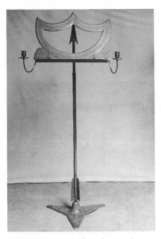

171 *above* Music stand, gilt metal, c.1810, the support is in the form of an arrow and the head a bow. (Harris)

172 *above* Dumb waiter, mahogany, c.1740, on a tripod base carved to resemble eagle legs. The supports between the trays are carved with acanthus. (Mallett)

173 *below* Tea kettle stand, mahogany, c.1760, on square-section reeded legs and brackets of pierced fret between these and the top. (Harris)

174 *below* Candelabra stands, carved and gilt, c.1775, in neo-classical taste decorated with rams' heads connected by festoons of bell flowers. The legs terminate in hoof feet and the stretchers are decorated with urn finials. (Hotspur)

also enabled conversation to be carried on during the meal without the restraint that might have to be exercised if servants were present.

KETTLE STANDS

These are closely associated with the rise in popularity of tea drinking. The earliest examples probably date from the end of the seventeenth century but they were not common until the mid-eighteenth century. The usual type is illustrated in plate 173. The kettle and its heater would be placed on top of the stand, the raised edge to the top being designed to protect the flame of the heater from draughts. The slide beneath the top, when extended, was intended to take the teapot. An alternative type of kettle stand was made in the mid-eighteenth century in the form of a miniature tea table with a tripod base and a top with a piecrust edge or gallery. This would be similar in size to the reproduction tables offered today in many furniture stores as 'wine tables', though for obvious reasons it would not have the tooled leather top found on modern pieces.

CANDLE AND LAMP STANDS

These were designed to supplement the fixed lighting of a room and first appeared in the Restoration period. Most existing examples are very elaborate, indicating their important place in the setting of reception rooms. Such stands usually consist of a shaped and carved centre support on a tripod base, with a flat surface at the top that is often surrounded by a low upturned edge. Plate 174 shows the type favoured in the Adam period. The single support common in the period before 1760 has been rejected in favour of three extended legs ending in hoof feet. The neo-classical influence is shown in the urns surmounting the central stretchers, the rams' heads and the festoons of husks, all favourite Adam devices. This example, like many late eighteenth-century stands, is gilded. A wide range of similar stands or pedestals were made for the display of porcelain, urns and busts or statuary.

WINE COOLERS AND CELLARETS

Before c. 1730 most wine coolers appear to have been of metal, and finer examples were made of silver. In the later half of the eighteenth century, however, mahogany wine cisterns lined with lead, usually set on short feet, appear to have become usual. Most large residences had an ice house in the grounds in which ice could be stored and this was placed in the wine cistern to cool the bottles needed for immediate use. Closely associated with wine coolers and often of similar shape are cella-

175 *above* Cellaret, mahogany, *c.*1770, of octagonal shape and brass bound. (Harris)

176 *below* Knife boxes, mahogany with inlay and banding of satinwood, boxwood and ebony, *c.*1775. (Victoria & Albert Museum)

177 *below* Tea caddies, late eighteenth century, of various woods, the lower one in the centre being veneered with tortoiseshall. (Spink)

rets, which were designed for the storage of bottles. They are fitted with a lid and are not lead lined. The hexagonal cellaret shown in plate 175 is typical of the plainer Georgian examples, though Adam's neo-classicism and later Regency taste resulted in designs representing classical cisterns and sarcophagi.

KNIFE BOXES

Boxes specially designed for the storage of cutlery appear to have been produced at least as early as the first half of the seventeenth century, but examples are rare until the second half of the eighteenth century, when two basic types make their appearance. The most common has a serpentine front and a sloping lid, which is often inlaid with a star. Narrow bands of chequer inlay frequently decorate both the exterior and the interior of the box. Knives and forks were inserted, handles upwards at the rear of the box, while spoons with their bowls upwards were placed at the front (plate 176). As early as the 1780s the trade of knife-box making appears to have been largely carried on by craftsmen specializing in this field.

The second type of knife box owed its popularity to the Adam taste and was vase shaped. The top could be lifted along a central pillar support and had a catch to hold it in the open position. The cutlery was then inserted vertically in slots arranged in concentric circles round the central support. Knife boxes were usually produced in pairs and the vase-shaped type was often made in conjunction with pedestals (see pp. 103, 104).

TEA CADDIES AND TEAPOYS

When tea was first imported into Britain it was expensive (an advertisement of 1665 records a price range from 16s to 50s a pound). Prices had fallen slightly by the first half of the eighteenth century but remained relatively high because of the import duty imposed on the commodity. The term caddy (derived from a corruption of the word *kati*—a Chinese measure of about a pound) is not used until the end of the eighteenth century, and Thomas Chippendale in the *Director* showed designs for what he called 'tea chests'. Before *c.* 1800 caddies were often small, with one or more compartments lined with metal foil. Larger and more elaborate examples have loose containers (sometimes of silver) to provide storage space for more than one type of tea and compartments for teaspoons. After *c.* 1800 many caddies adopted a sarcophagus shape and some had two wooden boxes inside with hinged lids for tea storage and a central well for a glass mixing bowl to enable the two types of tea to be blended or for the

178 *left* Long-case clock, walnut with Anglo-Dutch floral marquetry decoration, *c.*1690, fitted with an eight-day hour striking mechanism by Edward Faulbury, London. (Harris)

179 *below* Long-case clock, mahogany case with carved enrichment, swan-neck pediment and ogee bracket feet, *c.*1770. Eight-day hour striking mechanism with lunar dial in the arch by John Woollenden, Royton. (Harris)

storage of sugar. Despite the drastic fall in the price of tea in the nineteenth century this type of caddy with a lockable lid continued to be produced well into the Victorian period.

Caddies make an interesting subject for collecting. They are made both in metal and wood, the latter being covered with skin (shagreen), painted, inlaid or veneered with tortoiseshell (plate 177). Victorian examples were produced in Tunbridge ware, a mosaic of end-grain wood marquetry in which elaborate pictures of flowers, butterflies and views, mainly of the Tunbridge Wells area, were produced. Unfortunately tea caddies found today have often had their interiors gutted or have some parts missing. Replacement caddy bowls are very difficult to find and they vary considerably in size.

Teapoys were made in the first half of the nineteenth century and consist of an enlarged tea caddy, often with four tea canisters and two bowls, with a pillar support and platform base designed to stand on the floor.

(An equally interesting object for collecting is the workbox, which often follows similar stylistic forms to the caddies but is larger. These are again of much greater value if the interior fittings are complete.)

CLOCKS

To provide detailed information on clock mechanisms would be inappropriate in a book on furniture, but clearly long-case clocks are a major focus of attention in a furnishing scheme and involve considerable skill on the part of the craftsman responsible for the case.

The long-case clock was made possible by the development of the pendulum by the Dutch mathematician Christian Huygens in 1657, though subsequently in 1666 an Englishman, Dr Robert Hooke, demonstrated the advantage of the long pendulum beating once a second and this type soon became standard. This, coupled with the invention of the anchor escapement, made the long-case clock a successful and accurate timepiece. The weights that drove the clock were enclosed in a trunk instead of being exposed to view, as in the older lantern clocks. In the late Stuart and early Georgian periods English clockmakers such as Thomas Tompion, Daniel Quare, the Knibb family, Edward East, Joseph Windmills, George Graham and John Harrison gave England the lead in this field. Clocks were clearly regarded as objects of prime importance by their owners and clock cases were decorated with elaborate marquetry in many instances. The clock in plate 178 shows the Anglo-Dutch floral marquetry typical of the period 1670 to 1690. The case has an aperture in the trunk doors so that the movement of the pendulum could be observed, a

180 *above* Bracket clock, mahogany case with gilt embellishments and finials, *c.*1770. Eight-day hour striking mechanism by Benjamin Ward, London Road, Southwark, with strike/silent control in the arch. (Harris)

181 *above right* Bracket clock, mahogany case with brass inlay, *c.*1805. An eight-day timepiece is fitted but no maker's name is indicated. (Private collection)

182 *right* Wheel barometer, mahogany case, *c.*1840, by D'Angelo & Co, Winchester, fitted with hygrometer, detachable thermometer, convex mirror and level. (Private collection)

common feature in many seventeenth- and early eighteenth-century clocks. The most common type of mechanism was one that operated for eight days on one winding and struck the hours only. An independent seconds dial can be seen at the top of the face and there is a square aperture for a calendar dial showing the day of the month at the bottom. A cheaper alternative much favoured by some country makers was the thirty-hour clock, which needed winding each day. Such clocks have no winding apertures showing through the dial but are wound up by pulling a rope or chain inside the trunk.

Clocks by London and the best provincial makers were usually supplied with cases veneered in walnut up to c. 1740 and mahogany thereafter, though japanned cases were popular as an alternative up to c. 1760. Some country makers used oak for cheaper clock cases and even important makers like Thomas Tompion occasionally used oak cases. The case of the clock shown in plate 179 is an example of fine provincial craftsmanship. Clock cases were obviously not made by the clockmaker whose name was engraved on the dial plate, but must in most cases have been produced in the vicinity of the town named on the dial. This particular clock has a feature found in many late eighteenth- and early nineteenth-century clocks: a dial in the arch showing the phases of the moon. The arch dial was introduced c. 1715, though square dials continued to be used on some later clocks. Dials up to c. 1780 were usually of brass, with a separate chapter ring which was silvered to make the hands show more distinctly. Some late eighteenth-century dials were completely silvered for this reason, but a cheaper solution to the problem of legibility was the use of iron dials painted white, or more rarely enamel dials. On painted dials the cast-brass spandrels in the corners of the dial and arch were replaced by decoration, at first usually of flowers but later with scenes, often of various rustic or exotic landscapes. Early nineteenth-century clocks, especially those produced in the north of England, had cases with very wide trunks and elaborate banding and turned and carved decoration. Such clock cases often show good workmanship but are not always so pleasing in design. They are associated with the growth in wealth of the middle classes in the industrial areas of Yorkshire and Lancashire during this first phase of the Industrial Revolution. Well before the end of the eighteenth century many clock components and even complete mechanisms were being produced in quantity to a standard pattern for the trade; thus with late eighteenth- and nineteenth-century clocks the names on the dials are in many cases merely those of clock assemblers and retailers.

Most long-case clocks produced after c. 1730 are of provincial manufacture, as the London trade was concentrating by this date on spring-driven table or bracket clocks. These had first appeared during the Restoration, following the use of the short pendulum in such clocks by the Dutch clockmaker Fromanteel in 1658. Bracket clocks were portable and could be fitted with a repeat mechanism operated by a cord at the back, which when pulled caused the clock to repeat the number of strikes for the last hour. This would have been of assistance during the night. Brass dials of a type similar to those used on long-case clocks but smaller were used (plate 180). Late Georgian and especially Regency clocks have white painted dials. Those on Regency clocks are round in shape and covered with a convex dial glass, while the cases are usually of mahogany decorated with brass marquetry and in many instances are surmounted by an ormolu finial (plate 181). From the middle of the eighteenth century, however, English clockmakers faced competition from French clocks that were being imported in large quantities from the second quarter of the nineteenth century. By the middle of the century they were dominating the domestic market.

BAROMETERS

Antique barometers are of two types:

1. The stick barometer which consists of a cistern filled with mercury from which a sealed glass tube projects vertically. Air pressure acting on the mercury forces it up the small bore tube but because of its relatively small movement a vernier scale was provided in order to obtain accurate readings. Barometers of this type were produced from the end of the seventeenth century, some by important clockmakers such as Thomas Tompion and Daniel Quare. A few early examples have a tube which is vertical for about 28in, then is bent almost to the horizontal. Straight tube stick barometers continued to be produced for domestic use until the last quarter of the nineteenth century.

2. The wheel barometer originated in the late seventeenth century in an attempt to magnify the relatively small movement of the mercury in the tube and display this on a large dial by means of a needle. It was hoped that this would enable more accurate readings to be obtained, but such barometers were rare until the very end of the eighteenth century, when the 'banjo' type was introduced from the Continent. This resulted in the first half of the nineteenth century in a wave of popularity for this type of instrument. Immigrant Italian craftsmen appear to have played a large part in the production of barometers of this kind. Cases were usually of mahogany, though rosewood was also used. The head of the barometer was

often decorated with a scrolled or broken pediment. Dials were of silvered brass with a brass bezel. Early nineteenth-century examples have a long tube thermometer mounted above the barometer dial, a flat dial glass and sometimes a level beneath. Later examples incorporate a hygrometer to indicate humidity, a shorter thermometer and a mirror above the barometer dial (plate 182). As with clocks of this period, the 'maker's' name on the barometer may merely indicate a retailer or an assembler of components. A number of barometers were produced in a standard form clearly intended for retailing with the words 'guaranteed accurate' replacing the maker's name on either side of the spirit level. Later Victorian examples have heavy mouldings or carving to the case, though barometers with basically 'Georgian' styling were still listed in the catalogue of Negretti & Zamba in the late 1860s. The mercury barometer fell out of favour in the late nineteenth century because of the introduction of the anaeroid type. These were based on the action of pressure on a box containing a vacuum which activated the recording hand. They were less cumbersome and avoided the chance of mercury being spilt from the barometer.

6 Furniture Timbers

WE HAVE no space for a full list of the wide range of timbers used in the past by British furniture makers, but certain timbers such as oak, walnut, mahogany, satinwood and rosewood are frequently employed and it is essential that the novice should learn to recognise them at an early date. Other timbers are used more rarely or employed mainly for marquetry or banding and are more difficult to identify. Timber recognition can never be adequately achieved from printed descriptions and it is essential to visit a museum where the furniture exhibits are well labelled or described in a guide. The Victoria and Albert Museum in London, the Lady Lever Art Gallery at Port Sunlight or Temple Newsam House at Leeds are suitable places for studying furniture timbers at first hand. Even with common timbers different characteristics can result from alternative methods of converting the tree into planks (e.g. tangent-sawn and quarter-sawn oak) or from timber obtained from different parts of the tree.

1500–1660

Throughout this period the predominant furniture timber was oak. Most of this was grown in England, but some was imported from the Baltic area and this was favoured for the better grades of furniture. In the latter part of the sixteenth century inlay was popular with native woods such as bog oak, holly, sycamore, poplar, beech, ash, yew and fruit woods being used. In the late sixteenth and early seventeenth centuries walnut must have been used in increasing quantities, for finer pieces of furniture as it is frequently mentioned in contemporary inventories. In his *Naturall Historie* (1626) Bacon mentions the virtues of walnut as a wood for tables, cupboards and desks, but as it is less durable than oak and subject to worm attack its survival rate is low. This also applies to certain native timbers such as elm, which was used for table tops. Ash and beech were employed for chairs, while some turned chairs were made from yew.

1660–1730

During this period walnut became the predominant wood for furniture and was usually used as a veneer on case furniture and in the solid for chair and table legs. Deal from the Baltic was used for most carcases as it was found that the veneers adhered to this more satisfactorily than to oak. Walnut trees are known to have been grown at various places in the south of England, for example by Francis Slydolf of Mickleham in Surrey and Sir Robert Claydon at Marden in Kent, but the supply was insufficient to meet the demand. Imports came from the Continent, timber from Grenoble in France being particularly favoured. The severe havoc caused to the trees in Central Europe by the hard winter of 1709 restricted the supply of timber after this date, but a darker walnut (*juglans nigra*) was imported from the American colony of Virginia in increasing quantities from the end of the seventeenth century.

In the period following the Restoration 'oyster'-work of walnut, olive or laburnum was much in favour. This used transverse veneers cut from a small branch which repeated a circular grain pattern. By the beginning of the eighteenth century burr-walnut from protrusions near the base of the trunk was favoured because of its irregular and intricate veining.

Native woods such as oak, ash and elm continued to be used by provincial makers, some of whom still worked with the old frame and panel type of construction. A few surviving pieces of furniture from the late seventeenth century are veneered in mulberry or kingwood (an imported Brazilian timber similar in appearance to rosewood and known in the late seventeenth century as 'princes wood').

1730–70

Although walnut continued to be used after 1730 for some cabinets, chests of drawers, bureaux and clock cases it was unusual by 1750. Some native timbers were used by country makers. Apart from these exceptions, however, the period is dominated by mahogany, which was used at first in the solid for chairs and tables and later (from *c.* 1750) as a veneer on case furniture. Supplies were obtained initially from the Spanish West Indian islands of Puerto Rico and San Domingo (referred to as Spanish mahogany), the wood being dark in colour, close grained and lacking in figure. From *c.* 1750 Cuban timbers were favoured. These were redder in colour and showed a much more pronounced grain pattern, producing attractive curls and flare. They were used for veneers. Late in the eighteenth century wood from Honduras (Baywood) was imported, this being a lighter wood which was inferior in figure to the Cuban variety and was often used either in the solid or for inferior work. Mahogany had a virtual monopoly of fashionable furniture to *c.* 1770. Although this dominance was challenged at various periods in the late eighteenth and nineteenth centuries very substantial quantities of mahogany continued to be used up to the First World War. Today mahogany comes largely from African sources (Sapele, Utile) and differs considerably in appearance from earlier timber.

1770–1830

With the revival of interest in marquetry that began in the 1770s a lighter base wood was favoured. Satinwood was therefore frequently employed, the earliest supplies coming from the West Indies, though East Indian timber was also imported from 1780. The East Indian variety was a rather inferior wood which did not show its grain to the same effect as the West Indian type when polished. Satinwood was almost invariably used as a veneer. As originally finished, satinwood furniture was a light golden-yellow tone which as time has passed has mellowed to the rich honey shade that is familiar today in furniture of this period. Satinwood had fallen from popularity by *c.* 1800 but it was resuscitated in the second half of the nineteenth century under the influence of a revived interest in late eighteenth-century design.

Brazilian rosewood was used in the late eighteenth century for marquetry and banding purposes and from *c.* 1800 it became a serious rival to mahogany. The chief characteristic of this wood is its rich deep brown colour with streaks and patches of black. It is particularly associated with the Regency period, during which dark lustrous woods were favoured. Rosewood continued to be extensively used in the first three decades of Victoria's reign.

A number of timbers with very distinct figures were used on a smaller scale for finer pieces during the Regency, such as amboyna from Indonesia, with its curls and knots similar in form to birds'-eye maple. This was used as a veneer. Calamander-wood from India and Ceylon and zebra-wood from Brazil, both showing distinctive bands and streaks, were also used in small quantities. These are distinctively Regency timbers and were little used outside this period.

The popularity of painted, lacquered and ebonized chairs in the late Georgian period made the use of beech more common in the fashionable furniture trade, though beech chairs in imitation of the fashionable Georgian styles were produced in country areas throughout the eighteenth century.

1830–70

Although mahogany and rosewood continued in favour in the early Victorian period, walnut now made a reappearance and by *c.* 1850 was being extensively used both in the solid for chairs and as a veneer on case furniture and table tops. The revival in popularity of marquetry work made walnut a more suitable alternative for this type of decoration than mahogany or rosewood. For furniture in the Gothic taste oak came back into fashion and was being extensively used by the 1860s. The increasing demand for 'art' furniture with its use of ebonized wood revived an interest in beech from the late 1860s, while the arts and crafts tradition fostered by William Morris also favoured the use of native timbers. The complex pattern of Victorian styles is reflected in the wide range of timbers used, both native and foreign. The growing strength of Britain as a trading nation is shown in the increasing imports of timber from both America and East Asia. North American pine was almost universally adopted for cheaper grades of furniture for servants and artisans and as a carcase wood for fashionable pieces. By the middle of the nineteenth century this yellow pine had almost completely ousted the red and white pine from the Baltic; its import in the eighteen years ending in 1841 was said to have averaged 9,634,776 cubic ft and the trade was employing three hundred vessels.

7 Important Furniture Designers and Craftsmen

Adam, Robert (1728–92)

A noted architect and designer of interiors in the neo-classical taste, which he played a paramount part in popularizing in Britain. He was the second son of William Adam, an important Edinburgh architect, and visited Italy on the grand tour (1754–8), where he saw the ruins of Herculaneum, then recently excavated, and was greatly influenced by the growing knowledge of the classical world revealed by such discoveries. Among his most important commissions were Osterley, Isleworth and Syon House, Brentford, in Middlesex, Kedleston Hall in Derbyshire, Kenwood in Highgate, London, and Harewood House, Nostell Priory and Newby Hall in Yorkshire. For many houses he was responsible for the design of furniture for the state rooms, mainly those pieces designed to harmonize with the wall decoration. Many of his original drawings have survived, the main collection being at the Soane Museum in London. Some designs were printed in the *Works in Architecture*, published in parts from 1773 by Robert and James Adam.

Bullock, George

An important Regency cabinet-maker who moved from Liverpool to London *c.* 1813 and established himself at 4 Tenterden St, Hanover Square. He supplied furniture to Sir Walter Scott (1816–18) and a number of his designs appeared in *Ackermann's Repository of Arts*. He was noted for his use of metal inlay.

Burges, William (1827–81)

A noted Victorian architect and designer. He made a study of medieval furniture and art and was responsible for the design of a number of pieces of dramatic painted pseudo-medieval furniture which he displayed at the 1862 International Exhibition. Some furniture was made to his designs for buildings of which he was the architect, including the Marquis of Bute's Castell Coch near Cardiff.

Channon, John (1711–83?)

A cabinet-maker noted for his use of gilt metal mounts. He worked in Exeter before setting up in London in 1737 at The Pavement, St Martin's Lane. A pair of mahogany bookcases at Powderham Castle in Devon are of his manufacture and are dated 1740. Other brass inlaid pieces of furniture, including a fine cabinet in the Victoria and Albert Museum, are attributed to this maker, who may have collaborated with Abraham Rontgen, a German craftsman working in London at this period and using similar techniques.

Chippendale, Thomas (1718–79)

A cabinet-maker and designer, born in Otley in Yorkshire, who moved to London and had established his own business by 1749. In 1753 he moved to 60 St Martin's Lane, where he carried on his business until his death in 1779. His fame rests to a large degree on the design book *The Gentleman and Cabinet-Maker's Director* (1754, 2nd edn 1755, 3rd edn 1762), which was the first British design book devoted entirely to furniture. The plates show a wide range of furniture in the Rococo styles that were popular at that period. The finest extant furniture produced by Chippendale was made from the 1760s onwards in the neo-classical style—the introduction of which in Britain owes much to Robert Adam. Chippendale furniture with the original bills can be seen at Nostell Priory, Harewood House, Burton Constable and Newby Hall in Yorkshire, Mersham-le-Hatch in Kent, Dumfries House in Ayrshire and Paxton House in Berwickshire.

Chippendale, Thomas Jnr (1749–1822)

A cabinet-maker and the eldest son of Thomas Chippendale. In 1779 he took his father's place in the partnership with Thomas Haig at 60 St Martin's Lane. When Haig withdrew from the business in 1796 he traded on his own account. Between 1795 and 1820 he supplied furniture to Sir Richard Colt Hoare at Stourhead in Wiltshire, and Lord Townshend at Rainham in Norfolk paid him £1,200 for 'work done' in 1819. The furniture at Stourhead is still in the house and illustrates the Regency taste that was then current.

Cobb, John (*d.* 1778)

A London cabinet-maker who worked in partnership with William Vile (*qv*) between 1750 and 1765 at 72 St Martin's Lane. After this he appears to have traded on his own. His name is associated particularly with fine marquetry commodes in the French manner, one of which he is known to have supplied to Paul Methuen at Corsham Court in Wiltshire.

Crace, J. G. & Sons

Important Victorian cabinet-makers who produced furniture in the Gothic style to the designs of A. W. N. Pugin (*qv*) from 1847 to 1851. They supplied furniture for the Houses of Parliament.

Gillow & Co

Certainly the oldest surviving firm of cabinet-makers in Britain. The history of the enterprise can be traced back to Robert Gillow, who was made a freeman of Lancaster in 1728. Lancaster, then a port of some consequence, was used to import American timbers and the town was to remain the main centre of production of the firm. In 1769 additional showrooms were set up at 176 Oxford Street in London. Gillow's were one of the first makers to mark their furniture regularly with a manufacturer's name, an impressed stamp reading either 'Gillows' or 'Gillows Lancaster' being used. Furniture was marked intermittently from the 1790s but regularly from *c.* 1820. A range of estimate books detailing the commissions undertaken can now be seen in the Westminster City Library. The company was active throughout the nineteenth century and the name is still carried on by Waring & Gillow, the furniture retailers.

Grendey, Giles (1693–1780)

A cabinet-maker of St John's Square, Clerkenwell. He appears, like Gillow's to have carried on a considerable export trade as well as supplying British patrons. He was elected master of the Joiners' Company in 1766. Some pieces of furniture of his manufacture have a paper label pasted on them indicating that they are of his production. Some other makers used the same means of marking their work, though any identification is the exception rather than the rule with English furniture.

Godwin, E. W. (1833–86)

An architect and designer noted particularly for furniture designed in ebonized wood under the influence of Japanese styles from the 1860s and made by the cabinet-maker William Watt of Grafton Street in London.

He also produced designs for other firms such as Collinson & Lock, Gillow and W. & A. Smee. His designs mark an important stage on the road towards the development of modern functional design.

Goodison, Benjamin (d. 1767)

One of the most important cabinet-makers of the first half of the eighteenth century, whose workshop was situated at The Golden Spread Eagle, Long Acre in London. He supplied furniture for the Royal Household as well as for patrons such as Lord Folkestone and the Earl of Leicester. He is believed to have worked closely with William Kent (qv), the leading architect of the first half of the eighteenth century.

Gumley, John (d. 1729)

A cabinet-maker and supplier of looking glasses whose address was the New Exchange, Strand, London. He is first recorded in 1694, and in 1705 had his own glass-manufacturing works in Lambeth. He is associated in the royal accounts from 1714 to 1725 with John Moore (qv) and a mirror frame carved with his name exists at Hampton Court in Middlesex. Another mirror of his manufacture is at Chatsworth in Derbyshire.

Hallett, William (1701–81)

A cabinet-maker trading firstly from Newport Street and then (from 1753) from St Martin's Lane in London. He supplied furniture to the Earl of Leicester (1737), Lord Folkestone (1737–40), the Earl of Cardigan (1745) and Horace Walpole (1755). He had a flourishing business and in 1745 bought the Canons estate at Whitchurch in Middlesex from the Duke of Chandos.

Hepplewhite, George (d. 1786)

Despite the familiarity of Hepplewhite's name little is known about him. He is reputed to have been apprenticed to Gillows (qv) at Lancaster but there is no firm evidence to support this theory. By 1760 he had established himself at Redcross Street, St Giles, Cripplegate in London, but there is no evidence to suggest that he was engaged in cabinet-making at this address. No piece of furniture is marked with his name and he is not mentioned in any surviving accounts or papers referring to the supply of furniture. He was therefore probably engaged solely in the design of furniture and particularly of chairs. On his death in 1786 his widow Alice carried on the business and two years later published her husband's designs under the title *The Cabinet-Maker and Upholsterer's Guide*. A second edition followed in

1789 and a third edition (revised and with additional designs) in 1794. Hepplewhite's book, with its nearly three hundred designs, was the largest and most comprehensive publication in this field since Chippendale's *Director* and clearly illustrates the strong influence of Adam's neo-classicism in commercial furniture design.

Holland & Co

One of the leading firms of Victorian cabinet-makers. They supplied furniture to the royal family, including much of that at Osborne House in the Isle of Wight. Other patrons included the Duke of Wellington and Sir Robert Peel and they were also given numerous government contracts. The firm first appears in the London directories *c.* 1815 as Taprell & Holland. In 1843 the title was changed to Holland & Sons and *c.* 1852 they appear to have united with the firm of Thomas Dowbiggin & Co, another maker of considerable reputation. From 1852 Holland's address was 23 Mount St, Grosvenor Square, London, from which Dowbiggin had been trading since 1825. Holland's ceased business in 1942.

Holland, Henry (1745–1806)

A leading neo-classical architect who carried out a number of commissions for the Prince of Wales including Carlton House and the first Royal Pavilion in Brighton as well as for other patrons. He was strongly influenced by French trends in architecture and interior design and the furniture supplied for his commissions clearly shows this. He had a considerable influence on early Regency furniture design. His style is seen at its best at Southill in Bedfordshire, which he began to redecorate for Samuel Whitbread, the brewer, in 1796.

Hope, Thomas (1769–1831)

A connoisseur, art collector and amateur designer who for his London house in Duchess St designed a range of furniture based on archeological precedent and using Roman, Greek and Egyptian forms and motifs. The furniture was designed to harmonize with the collection of classical antiquities displayed in the rooms. This furniture was illustrated in his book *Household Furniture and Interior Decoration* (1807) and was a great influence on design in the first two decades of the nineteenth century.

Ince, William and Mayhew, John

Founded a firm of cabinet-makers that was to enjoy a considerable reputation in the late Georgian period. They published a design book in parts from 1759 and in a collected edition in 1762 under the title of *The Universal System of Household Furniture*; this was the main rival to Chippendale's *Director*. At the date of publication their address was Broad Street, Carnaby Market in London, but from 1779 they were working from an address in Marshall Street, Carnaby Market. The firm continued to operate until *c.* 1810.

Jensen, Gerreit (active *c.* 1680–1715)

A royal cabinet-maker from the reign of Charles II to Queen Anne. His name also appears in records at Chatsworth in Derbyshire. He made use of metal inlay in some of his furniture, an innovation practised by André Charles Boulle, cabinet-maker to Louis XIV of France. Jensen also sold mirrors.

Johnson, Thomas (1714–78?)

A carver and designer in the Rococo style who worked from various London addresses. He started publishing designs for mirrors, *girandoles*, console tables and chimney pieces in 1755 and his collected designs were published in book form under the titles *One Hundred and Fifty New Designs* (1758 and 1761) and *A New Book of Ornament* (1760).

Kent, William (1686–1748)

The leading architect of the Early Georgian period, who produced a number of designs for furniture in connection with the house interiors for which he was responsible. Some of these were published in 1744 by his disciple John Vardy under the title *Some Designs of Mr. Inigo Jones and Mr. Wm. Kent* (1744). Furniture that he designed for the state rooms of large houses such as Holkham Hall in Norfolk incorporate boldly carved features inspired by the Italian baroque furniture that he had seen during his stay in Italy (1710–19)

Le Gaigneur, Louis

A French cabinet-maker who traded from 19 Queen St, Edgware Road in London during the Regency period. He specialized in buhl work (furniture decorated with marquetry of brass and tortoiseshell) and is known to have supplied furniture for the Prince of Wales to be used in Carlton House.

Linnell, John (*d.* 1796)

An important designer and cabinet-maker whose London address was 28 Berkeley Square. A large number of his designs were collected together after his death by C. H. Tatham (*qv*) and these are now preserved in the Victoria and Albert Museum. They bear testimony to the importance of his patrons. Linnell supplied furniture for a number of houses for which Adam was the architect, including Kedleston in Derbyshire, Shardeloes in Buckinghamshire, Croome Court in Worcestershire and Osterley in Middlesex. The William Linell who was working at the same address until his death in 1763 was his father.

Lock, Mathias

A carver and designer whose published designs clearly demonstrate the advance of the Rococo influence in English furniture design. His first publication was *A New Drawing Book of Ornaments* (1740) and this was followed by further published designs for sconces and tables in the 1740s. His *A New Book of Ornament* (1752) shows that he had fully mastered the Rococo style by this date, two years before the publication of Chippendale's *Director*. After this he published nothing further until 1768. This silence is one of the reasons for the theory that Lock was now producing designs for Chippendale, including those incorporated in the *Director* but this theory is now generally discredited. A number of unpublished drawings by Lock covering the period 1740 to 1765 can be seen in the Victoria and Albert Museum and these were no doubt produced in connection with his business as a carver, which he carried on at Nottingham Court, Castle Street, Long Acre in London and from 1752 from near Ye Swan in Tottenham Court Road.

Loudon, John Claudius (1783–1843)

An architect and landscape gardener who was a prolific writer. His most important work as far as the study of furniture is concerned is the *Encyclopaedia of Cottage, Farm & Villa Architecture & Furniture* (1833 and subsequent editions). Loudon produced the text but most of the pieces of furniture illustrated appear to have been drawn from the stock of W. F. Dalziel, a cabinet-maker of Great James Street in London. Loudon's work gives us a valuable insight into furniture design on the eve of the reign of Queen Victoria. A wide range of quality is represented, from pieces of considerable elegance to simple cottage furniture.

Manwaring, Robert

Little is known of this cabinet- and chair-maker whose premises were in the Haymarket in London, except that in 1765 he published *The Cabinet and Chair Maker's Real Friend and Companion*, which was followed in the next year by the *Chairmaker's Guide*, some of the designs in which are by other hands. Although the draughtsmanship in Manwaring's designs is defective they do display a marked originality.

Marot, Daniel (1663–1752)

An architect and designer of Huguenot extraction, who after studying as a designer under Le Pautre and in the establishment of André-Charles Boulle in France moved to Holland to become Master of Works to William of Orange. When William became king of England in 1688 Marot undertook a number of commissions in Britain, including work at Hampton Court. His collected designs, displaying the court taste of Louis XIV's France, were published in 1702. English furniture of this period shows Marot's influence, a good example being the Melville bed in the Victoria and Albert Museum.

Moore, James (d. 1726)

A royal cabinet-maker who worked in partnership with John Gumley (*qv*). The earliest known references to him date from 1708, when he was working for the Duke of Montagu. A table and stands at Hampton Court Palace are impressed with his name. He appears to have specialized in gilt furniture, especially tables, stands and chests with complex raised scroll patterning, often displaying the crests and coats of arms of his patrons.

Morris, William (1834–96)

An important Victorian designer, poet and radical. In 1861 he established the firm of Morris, Marshall Faulkner & Co to 'execute work in a thoroughly artistic and inexpensive manner' and to counter the low standards of design and craftsmanship that Morris saw in the commercial products of his day. Morris himself was little concerned with furniture design but the company produced both expensive 'state furniture' for individual commissions and a range of 'joiner-made or cottage furniture' in greater quantity and at lower prices. The main designer initially was Ford Madox Brown, while Philip Webb, the architect, was concerned with the design of much of the state furniture. Of the early commercial designs the most popular appear to have been the rush-seated Sussex chair and an adjustable upholstered armchair. The company was active until 1940 and from *c*. 1890 marked their name on furniture.

Pelletier, John

A Frenchman active in England from *c*. 1690 to 1710. He appears to have specialized in carved and gilt furniture and was one of the earliest producers in England in this field. He was associated with the furnishing of Hampton Court Palace and two sets of stands supplied by him can still be seen there.

Pugin, A. W. N. (1812–52)

An architect and designer particularly associated with the Gothic style. His father, Augustus Charles Pugin, worked as an architectural assistant to John Nash and produced furniture designs in the Gothic taste that were published in 1829 under the title *Gothic Furniture*. The Gothic furniture designs of A. W. N. Pugin differ fundamentally from those of his father, who used Gothic detail merely to decorate furniture of conventional late Regency style and construction. A. W. N. Pugin did however attempt to recapture the spirit of Gothicism by following medieval forms and craftsmanship. In 1835 he published a book of his furniture designs under the title *Gothic Furniture in the Style of the 15th Century*. His work had a very considerable effect on the interest in Gothic design in the Victorian period.

Seddon, George (1727–1801)

One of the most important cabinet-makers in London in the second half of the eighteenth century, he appears to have established his workshops in Aldersgate Street in about 1750. An account detailing the wide range of fine furniture available for sale is given by the German novelist Sophie von la Roche, who recorded a visit to the works in her diary in 1786. Seddon's supplied furniture to Somerset House from 1779. On the death of George Seddon the firm was carried on by his sons and continued to enjoy a high reputation until late in Victoria's reign. Between 1826 and 1830 they supplied furniture valued at £200,000 for Windsor Castle and much work in the Gothic style was produced for various patrons between 1860 and 1880.

Shearer, Thomas

Shearer contributed seventeen out of the twenty plates in *The Cabinet-Makers' London Book of Prices* (1788). This book was intended as an aid to both master and workman in calculating prices and piece-work rates, and continued in publication with alterations and additions (though under a different title) until 1866. Shearer's drawings reflect furniture being produced in the London cabinet trade in the 1780s and are thus in the style loosely described as 'Hepplewhite'. They are detailed and the draughtsmanship is of a high standard. Of Shearer himself little is known, but it is thought that he was a journeyman cabinet-maker in the employ of one of the main London master cabinet-makers.

Sheraton, Thomas (1751–1806)

A furniture designer and drawing teacher whose published designs are included in *The Cabinet Maker's and Upholsterer's Drawing Book* (1791–4, 2nd edn 1794, 3rd edn 1802), *The Cabinet Dictionary* (1803) and *The Cabinet-Maker, Upholsterer and General Artist's Encyclopaedia* (1805), of which the first is by far the most important. Before 1790, when he moved to London, Sheraton lived mainly in the Stockton area, where he was a Baptist preacher and pamphleteer. He was probably a cabinet-maker by trade but there is no evidence that he practised this trade in London, where he seems to have made a precarious living as an author, designer and drawing teacher.

Smith, George

An important Regency designer who in 1808 published one of the most comprehensive collections of furniture designs of this period under the title *A Collection of Designs for Household Furniture and Interior Design*. This book shows the influence of Thomas Hope's archaeological approach, but illustrates also designs in other styles including the Gothic and Chinese tastes. Smith described himself as "Upholder Extraordinary to His Royal Highness the Prince of Wales" but there is no evidence to date of his employment by the Royal Family and he does not appear to have practised the trade of upholsterer as a regular employment on his own behalf. A further collection of furniture designs reflecting late Regency styles was published in 1828 entitled *The Cabinet-Maker and Upholsterer's Guide*.

Tatham, Charles Heathcote (1771–1842)

An architectural assistant to Henry Holland (*qv*) who was sent to Rome so that he could supply drawings of classical architecture and art for Holland to use in his commissioned designs. In 1799 Tatham published *Etchings Representing the Best Examples of Ancient Ornamental Architecture*, a design book that proved a valuable quarry for furniture and other designers during the Regency period. The book was reissued in 1803, 1810, 1826 and 1843. His brother Thomas Tatham was head of the London cabinet-maker's Marsh & Tatham of Mount Street, who supplied considerable quantities of furniture for the Royal Pavilion in Brighton.

Vile, William (*d.* 1767)

A royal cabinet-maker who established himself at 72 St Martin's Lane in London. He supplied furniture for George, Prince of Wales, whose patronage continued after 1760, when he ascended the throne as George III. Authenticated work by William Vile is noted for its quality and particularly the standard of the carved decoration. From *c.* 1750 to his death in 1767 he carried on an extensive trade. For the later part of this period he was in partnership with John Cobb (*qv*).

The information given in this list concerns only a small number of known furniture-makers and designers. For a comprehensive list of London cabinet-makers active in the period 1660 to 1840 readers are referred to Sir Ambrose Heal, *The London Furniture Makers* (1953). References in this book are generally brief and further detail about the major designers, and illustrations of their work, can be found in Ralph Edwards and Margaret Jourdain, *Georgian Cabinet Makers*, 3rd edn (1955). For the Victorian period information is less extensive but the list in Elizabeth Aslin, *19th Century English Furniture* (1962) will prove useful. Information is coming to light the whole time and recent discoveries are often referred to in articles in such publications as *Apollo*, the *Burlington Magazine*, the *Connoisseur* and *Furniture History*. Generally speaking, there are no equivalent lists of provincial makers.

It is very unlikely that the makers of the bulk of English furniture will ever be identified. Furniture was rarely marked, though a few pieces are known with trade labels affixed, often in drawers; a few other makers stamped their name on their products. On some Victorian pieces such names may be those of retailers rather than manufacturers. Local directories, available at most large public libraries, will help to identify the approximate dates of working for cabinet-makers active from the late eighteenth century and later if they cannot be traced from other sources.

In houses where accounts and original furniture have been kept together it is possible to identify the maker with certainty. Thomas Chippendale and most leading makers did not mark their furniture and accounts existing in private houses are the only way in which such identification can be made.

8 Buying Antique Furniture

MANY READERS with an interest in the heritage of English crafts-manship will wish to acquire at least some items of antique furniture to enhance the appearance of their homes. Not only is it a joy to be sur-rounded by such items, but if they are chosen with discernment and cared for they will represent an investment that will gradually appreciate in value. The furnishing of a room with pieces of the same period has obvious appeal, but a mixture of antiques of various dates can also provide a pleasant setting. Furniture made from native timbers such as oak, beech, elm, yew and fruit woods, or from pine is particularly suitable for old country cottages. Such furniture of provincial manufacture is usually more modestly priced than that in fashionable imported timbers such as walnut, mahogany, satinwood or rosewood. This is particularly true of furniture made in the eighteenth and early nineteenth centuries.

A basic knowledge of period furniture can be obtained from books and reinforced by visits to museums and country houses. Sooner or later, however, will come the desire to own pieces oneself. The amount that one is prepared to spend and the degree of quality that one is prepared to accept will naturally dictate the source of supply. As with all collecting, the advice to buy the best that you can afford applies—choose a few items of good quality rather than many of a lesser standard. Against this however must, especially for the novice, be weighed the thought that if mistakes are going to be made they should be as inexpensive as possible. Much valuable experience can be gained from the purchase of relatively inexpensive pieces, even if such items have to be disposed of at a later date and replaced with pieces of higher quality. For the complete novice who still feels the urge to seek 'quality' pieces at bargain prices, a word of cau-tion is necessary. If an item is cheaply priced there may be a good reason for it: remember at this stage that the dealer almost certainly knows considerably more than you do.

Antique shops will probably be one of the main sources from which furniture will be acquired. Businesses in this field vary greatly however in the extent and the quality of their stock. If the buyer is seeking furniture of quality of the Georgian period or earlier, this will be more expensive and this area is strewn with many pitfalls for the novice bargain-hunter (see pp. 153–6). Such pieces should be bought only from dealers specializing in antique furniture of the period concerned. If the novice is not personally acquainted with a local dealer it is advisable for him to seek out a member of the British Antique Dealers' Association, who will be prepared to guarantee the authenticity of any piece that he sells; such members value their reputation too highly to sell a piece of doubtful parentage and will point out any repairs or alterations that have been made. The buyer will have to pay the fair market price for the item, but it may well be cheaper in the long run than to buy a 'bargain' that proves not to be what it seems. Addresses of dealers who are members of The British Antique Dealers' Association can be obtained by writing to their headquarters at 20 Rutland Gate, London SW7.

The bargain-hunting instinct often appears to be inbuilt in the antique collector. Most shops advertising antiques have some furniture, usually Victorian or later, reproductions or country pieces. Occasionally something of higher quality will be purchased, but as such dealers have contacts with other members of the trade who are better able to dispose of items of this kind, they are liable to be passed on quite quickly. Prices in the smaller general antique shops will often be lower than those asked by the specialist, but the risks are greater as the dealer selling a wide variety of antiques will be less familiar with the better pieces. He may however provide a source for the collector with a restricted budget seeking pieces of lower quality. Some dealers do most of their business with other members of the trade and may provide a profitable source of supply for the more knowledgeable collector willing to take furniture 'in the rough' and carry out minor renovations himself. The business premises of such dealers do not have the elegance and attraction of those of the main street or village dealer, but prices may be very reasonable, often little above auction prices. Junk shops and secondhand furniture shops, which were at one time useful hunting-grounds, today have little of merit in most cases and the few good pieces are unlikely to be sold for bargain prices.

If a specific piece of antique furniture is required a tour of the antique dealers in a large town or within a reasonable radius from one's home will not only establish the fair price for the article required but will also provide a range from which to select. Antique dealers are always willing to allow prospective buyers to inspect their stock and are prepared to answer customers' questions. Condition will always be a factor in making a decision to purchase. Slight damage may be acceptable, but the skill of a good antique restorer has to be paid for and such work cannot be hurried if a satisfactory result is to be achieved. Furniture that is structurally unsound should be avoided, unless you have the skill to put it right yourself, but missing brass handle drops or keyhole escutcheon plates are less important as a wide range of reproductions are available from suppliers of fittings to the cabinet trade, with the result that many types can be matched. Woodworm can be cured if it is not serious, but it should be tackled immediately with one of the proprietary woodworm killers; pine, beech and other softer woods are most vulnerable.

Auctions provide another source of supply but must be approached with caution by the novice. Since the introduction of the Trade Descriptions Act auctioneers, country auctioneers especially, have tended to be rather vague in their descriptions. Only when they are absolutely certain will they use terms like 'Georgian' or 'Regency'. The terms 'Chippendale', 'Hepplewhite' or 'Sheraton' in a catalogue refer to late eighteenth-century furniture in the style of the designers indicated. Furniture thought to be a reproduction of a later date will usually be described as 'Chippendale style', 'Hepplewhite style' and so on. The prospective buyer is often left with no option but to make up his own mind. Before attempting to buy at an auction lots should be carefully examined on the viewing day to see if they are structurally sound and confirmation of their authenticity should be sought by opening drawers and cupboards and examining the underneath of chairs and tables (see pp. 153–6). It is advisable to assess the value of the desired item in advance by regular attendance at sales and careful recording of prices over a period before making any attempt to bid oneself. If time does not permit this, the auctioneer or senior porter in the saleroom may be able to provide an accurate estimate. They may also be willing to act for buyers unable to attend the sale. A porter acting for a buyer in this way is entitled to a gratuity for his trouble if the bid is successful. Many pieces at an auction sale fetch prices slightly lower than equivalent items bought from an antique dealer, and a few are knocked down for substantially less. At every sale there are also a number of pieces that fetch considerably more than their true value because two or more bidders are determined to acquire them. It is only too easy to panic in a saleroom, so establish the true value of the lot before the sale begins and make sure that you keep rigidly to the limit you have set yourself. To the cost of the article in the saleroom must also be added the charge for delivery by carrier, whereas some antique dealers will provide free delivery locally.

9 Fakes, Frauds and Reproductions

THE INCREASING DEMAND for antique furniture and consequent rise in prices makes skilled faking worth practising, and therefore a number of general points to be considered when purchasing are listed in this section. It must be emphasised, however, that good fakes and altered pieces are often difficult to detect and need a trained eye backed by years of experience. The greater the familiarity with genuine period furniture the less likelihood of being deceived; a careful examination of pieces in museums and collections open to the public is recommended. No book can provide a substitute for experience.

The main groups into which faked or altered furniture may be grouped are:

Improved pieces: genuine pieces of period furniture that have been altered or added to with a view to passing them off as items belonging to an earlier period or of finer quality.

Transformations: the alteration of pieces of period furniture which are in lesser demand, e.g. Georgian wardrobes (linen presses), into others where the demand is greater, e.g. book or display cases.

Marriages: e.g. the addition of a bookcase to a bureau to make a bureau bookcase of greater value than the two component parts.

Reduction in size of large pieces of furniture so that they will more readily find a market.

Reproductions may also provide difficulty. Modern reproductions are not difficult to detect for not only do they lack the wear that would be expected on genuine period furniture but they are often made of different timbers from those used in the period concerned and need to be stained to approximate to the correct colouration. The result is usually a bright, sickly finish that would deceive nobody who was familiar with genuine period furniture. Reproductions of an earlier period may, however, prove more difficult. From the 1860s a number of eighteenth-century styles were reproduced and although some firms like Wright & Mansfield marked their work most did not. Such furniture may now be antique in its own right and will show many of the signs of age of the genuine article. A considerable amount of inlaid furniture in Georgian styles was made in the first decade of the twentieth century, but the use of marquetry is excessive in many cases, and out of keeping with the work of the eighteenth-century craftsman. The Adam/Hepplewhite style in particular attracted the Edwardian craftsman.

When assessing the genuineness of furniture certain factors are of particular importance.

SIGNS OF WEAR

A piece of furniture that has been in use over a long period of time will be marked by knocks and abrasions. The bottoms of drawers and drawer runners will show wear and the bottoms of table and chair legs extensive scratch marks and dents. Attempts have been made to simulate wear but fakers are at times over-enthusiastic and bruising may be far too regular and wear in the wrong place. Furniture bought 'in the rough', provided the repairs needed are not too extensive, may well prove a better buy than pieces in pristine restored condition that may have been tampered with.

PATINATION

Constant polishing of a piece of furniture over a period of time will result in a finish that it is difficult for the faker to imitate successfully. Pieces of furniture may well have been left in places where the sun has faded the wood but the tops of drawer fronts and the wood under brass handle plates will still be darker because the sun will not have affected it. This gives a good clue to age. Chairs are likely to have been picked up many times in their lives and may show evidence of this in darker patches under the seat frame or open arms. Drawer sides can also be expected to be darker near the front where they have been handled and where dust could penetrate.

STAIN

Stain has rarely been used on fashionable furniture and pieces showing white edges where polishing has worn away the stained surface are suspect. Stain used on the undersides of furniture to darken the wood is also a likely sign of faking because this was never practised in the past. Some chairs of the Georgian period were stained to imitate mahogany or rosewood, but such pieces will have lost much of their original stain and will have acquired a fine patination.

BRASS FITTINGS

These are readily available today and much Victorian furniture that started off its life with wooden knobs is now fitted with reproduction plates and handles to give it a superficial Georgian appearance. An examination of the interior of the drawers will show clearly that an alteration has been effected because the hole into which the wooden knob has been fitted will clearly show. Reproduction brass fittings made today are usually treated to make polishing unnecessary whereas old fittings will tend to go dull and greenish if not constantly polished.

UNEXPOSED WOOD

Often the back, underneath or inside of faked furniture is instructive and if new wood is found it should be treated with suspicion. It may represent a repair but it may equally well indicate a major alteration in size or function. Nails and screws that have been in position for a considerable time will have rusted and permanently marked the surrounding wood.

VENEERS

Modern veneers are knife cut and wafer thin, whereas antique furniture will in most cases have saw cut veneers that are between $\frac{1}{16}$ in to $\frac{1}{8}$ in thick. Chipped veneer or exposed edges will show if the thicker saw cut veneer has been used. The use of oak for the interior of drawers or carcases suggests age, though much pine was also used for carcase construction of antique furniture.

CARVING

This should be deep and crisp and stand well clear of the surface. Shallow carving may well be a sign of later improvement. Mouldings are sometimes added to improve pieces, but the regularity of modern machine-produced moulding usually gives them away.

JOINTS

All joints on antique furniture will be hand made and will show minor irregularities as a consequence. Hand-cut dovetail joints will usually have thin pins and a scribe mark will run down the side of the drawer to mark their termination. Machine-cut dovetails will have larger pins, equal in size to the tails between them and no scribe mark will be shown.

Those who wish to pursue this matter of fakes are advised to consult two recently published books:

Charles H. Hayward, *Antique or Fake* (London 1970).

W. Crawley, *Is It Genuine?* (London 1971).

Both contain excellent photographs that emphasize the main points to look out for when assessing the age and originality of a piece of furniture. Mr Hayward's book is particularly informative about the types of construction used by craftsmen in the past.

Appendix 1
Further Reading

GENERAL

The best reference work on English furniture to 1830 is P. Macqoid and R. Edwards, *Dictionary of English Furniture* (London 1954). This three-volume work, abridged but still very comprehensive, was reissued in 1964 (edited by R. Edwards) under the title *Shorter Dictionary of English Furniture*. Both of these are relatively expensive, but they can be consulted in most reference libraries. At the other end of the price scale is Ralph Fastnedge, *English Furniture Styles 1500–1830* (1955), a Penguin paperback that successfully relates changing furniture styles to the society of the day. A comparison of styles in other European countries and the United States with those of Britain is made in Helena Hayward (ed.), *World Furniture* (London 1965).

SPECIFIC PERIODS IN ENGLISH FURNITURE
Before 1660
S. W. Wolsey & R. W. P. Luff, *Furniture in England – The Age of the Joiner* (London 1968)

Georgian
R. Edwards & M. Jordain, *Georgian Cabinet Makers*, 2nd edn, (London 1955)

A. Coleridge, *Chippendale Furniture* (London 1966)

E. T. Joy, *Chippendale* (London 1971)

R. Fastnedge, *Sheraton Furniture* (London, 1962)

C. Musgrave, *Adam, Hepplewhite and Other Neo-Classical Furniture* (London 1966)

C. Musgrave, *Regency Furniture* (London 1965)

M. Jourdain, *Regency Furniture*, (rev. edn (London 1965)

Victorian

Elizabeth Aslin, *19th-Century English Furniture* (London 1962)

R. W. Symonds & B. Whineray, *Victorian Furniture* (London 1962)

INDIVIDUAL ITEMS OF FURNITURE

E. T. Joy, *The Country Life Book of Chairs* (London 1967)

G. Wills, *English Looking Glasses* (London 1965)

E. Burton, *The Long-Case Clock* (London 1964)

A series of booklets issued by the Victoria and Albert Museum contain illustrations of the pieces in the possession of the museum, with full descriptions and a short introductory section. Among the titles issued are:

English Chairs, 3rd edn (1970)

English Desks and Bureaux (1968)

English Cabinets (1964)

Chests of Drawers and Commodes (1960)

Tables (1968)

PERIODICALS

Important articles on the history of English, Continental and American furniture appear in *Apollo*, the *Burlington Magazine* and the *Connoisseur* from time to time. The serious enthusiast will also consider joining the Furniture History Society, whose members receive the annual journal *Furniture History* and in addition may enjoy lectures and visits organized by the society. Details of membership may be obtained from the Assistant Secretary, Department of Woodwork, Victoria and Albert Museum, London SW7.

Popular magazines concerned with antiques and collecting that contain articles on furniture include:

Antique Collector (alternate months)

Antique Dealer and Collector's Guide (monthly)

Antiques (alternate months)

Art and Antiques Weekly (weekly)

Appendix 2
Glossary of terms

Acanthus

Stylized leaf carving frequently found on furniture during the eighteenth and nineteenth centuries, though earlier examples are also known. The origin of this form of decoration is to be found in classical architecture, for instance on the capitals of the Corinthian order (plates 22, 23, 70).

Anthemion

A stylized form of the honeysuckle flower taken from classical sources. It was much used as a form of decoration in the furniture of the Adam period, where it can be found in marquetry, painted or applied in the form of metal mounts (plate 88).

Apron

A piece of wood, added for decorative purposes to the base of case furniture, especially of the late eighteenth and early nineteenth centuries, an example is the shaped apron beneath bow-fronted chests of drawers of this period. Aprons may also be found below chair seats and table friezes (plate 114).

Arabesque

A complex pattern of intertwined stylized foliate stems or lines. Carved decoration in this form was used in the late sixteenth and early seventeenth centuries (plate 126) and arabesque marquetry is found on cabinets and clock cases from the period 1690 to 1720.

Astragal

A term used to describe the glazing bars of cabinets and bookcases (plates 129, 130, 131, 136, 137).

Ball and Claw

A type of carved foot frequently used in the early eighteenth century on chairs and tables and representing a claw clutching a ball (plates 70, 72).

Baluster turning

Turning of an ornamental nature used on chair and table legs or supports, especially in early oak furniture of the sixteenth and seventeenth centuries (plates 58, 59).

Banding

The application of a border veneer of the same or a different wood on the top of tables or chests of drawers and on drawer or cupboard fronts of all case furniture. Where the grain is at right angles to that of the main veneer wood it is said to be cross-banded (plates 97, 107, 108, 117).

Baroque

A term used to denote the prevailing style of architecture and interior decoration in Britain in the later part of the seventeenth century and the first decades of the eighteenth. It was introduced from the Continent, where among other countries it flourished in Italy, France and Austria. The Baroque style makes full use of the dramatic effect to be obtained by massed detail, flowing lines and the use of light and shade (plates 66, 67).

Berlin Wool work

Embroidery material used extensively in the early Victorian period for upholstery or for covering screens. The earliest materials and patterns were of German origin and they were imported in considerable quantities from 1831 by a Mr Wilks of Regent Street in London. By 1840 no fewer than fourteen thousand different patterns had been imported or published in Britain. The usual subjects were floral designs or birds (especially parrots), though historical, religious or romantic pictures also provided themes (plates 52, 53).

Blind fret

Used to describe carved work similar to fretting (*qv*), where the wood is not pierced (plate 27).

Bolection moulding

A moulding of ogee section (convex above, concave below) used as a surround for a panel. Much favoured in Victorian furniture (plate 149).

Bombé

A term of French origin used to describe the swelling outline of mid-eighteenth-century commodes.

Bun foot

A foot of elliptical form used on case furniture in the late seventeenth century and also in the early Victorian period (plates 105, 134).

Cabochon

A polished, circular, convex ornament framed with additional carving, found particularly on the knees of Early Georgian chairs.

Cabriole leg

A leg used on chairs, tables and stands, particularly in the early Georgian period. The leg is S-shaped and usually terminates in a hoof, paw, ball and claw or scroll foot. The leg shape was revived in the early Victorian period, when it was used extensively on chairs, mainly with buckle or balloon backs. The usual Victorian termination is the scroll foot (plates 18, 19, 20, 22, 23, 25, 26, 33, 34, 49, 50, 51, 70, 71, 72).

Canted

A term used for the chamfered edges of a piece of furniture, usually one of case construction such as a chest of drawers. Found on early and mid-eighteenth-century pieces (plates 109, 110).

Cartouche

A decorative frame, usually enclosing a coat of arms or other device, used to decorate the cornices of beds and large case furniture (plate 155).

Caryatid

A carved female figure used as a support or ornament, especially on furniture of the late sixteenth century (plate 122).

Case construction (or carcase construction)

A method of construction using flat panels of wood dovetailed into each other and usually veneered with another wood. This type of construction took over from the frame and panel in *c.* 1660 and became almost universal for all cabinet work.

Chimera

A winged creature of Greek mythology killed by Bellerophon. The mask or monopodia (*qv*) form was used as a carved decorative feature in furniture of the Regency period.

Chinese Chippendale

A style using pseudo-oriental forms and motifs popular in the mid-eighteenth century. Chippendale illustrated furniture in this style in the *Director* but he was not the only exponent and was not the originator of the style (plates 30, 130, 164).

Chip carving

Shallow carving often of poor quality, executed with chisel and gouge. Practised from the Middle Ages to the end of the seventeenth century (plate 59).

Cluster column legs

Legs carved to represent a cluster of bamboo rods; used on some furniture in the Chinese and Gothic tastes in the mid-eighteenth century.

Cock bead

A flat bead with rounded front added to the edge of drawer fronts from the early eighteenth century to well into the nineteenth century (plates 111, 114, 115).

Cornice

A moulding applied to the top of a piece of case furniture or a bed often projecting forward of the front (plates 108, 109, 121, 123, 127, 131, 135).

Console table

An ornamental table supported on legs or a carved figure, often of an eagle, which must be fixed to a wall for support (plates 75, 77).

Cresting

Carved decoration added to late sixteenth- and early seventeenth-century chairs above the top rail of the back. Some late seventeenth-century mirrors and cabinets on stands also had crestings (plates 5, 161).

Dentil moulding

An architectural cornice moulding used on large case furniture of the

Georgian period and consisting of small rectangular protrusions resembling teeth (from the French *dent*, 'tooth') (plates 123, 129).

Dished

A term used for a chair seat that has been recessed to take a cushion; a feature often found on early seventeenth-century and some later country-made chairs (plates 10, 12). Depressions can also be found on eighteenth century card tables for coins or counters and supper tables for plates to which this term can be applied.

Dowel

A peg used to hold a mortice and tenon joint in furniture of frame and panel construction. Circular dowels were also used on some late Victorian chairs to joint the members of chair seat frames (figures 1, 3).

Escritoire

A writing cabinet with a fall front usually dating from the late seventeenth century. Contemporary inventories appear to use the term 'scriptor' for these pieces (cf. secretaire).

Finial

A decorative motif of turned or carved wood or cast metal or ivory surmounting a piece of furniture (plates 135, 181), or at the intersection of stretchers in the case of tables or chairs, especially of the late seventeenth century (plates 16, 19).

Fluting

Semi-circular concave grooves similar to those found on classical columns (plates 109, 110, 123, 126).

Frame and panel construction

The usual method of furniture construction for fashionable pieces until the mid-seventeenth century and continued to the early eighteenth century in some provincial areas. Chamfered panels were inserted into rebates on a framework formed with the use of mortice and tenon joints (figures 1, 3).

Fret

A border or cresting of decorative motifs where the wood has been pierced through (plates 78, 79). The term is also used for the brass trellis popular in the Regency period (plate 148).

Frieze

A border often decorated with carved, marquetry or painted ornament below the cornice of a piece of case furniture (plate 136) or below the top of a table (plates 71, 73).

Gadrooning (or nulling)

A carved edge ornament of repetitive convex form (plate 56).

Gesso

A layer of whiting and parchment size applied to furniture or picture frames before gilding.

Gilding

The application of gold leaf to a piece of furniture. Two methods were used: water gilding, the usual professional method, which made it possible to burnish the object; and oil gilding (plates 66, 67).

Guilloche

A classical architectural border pattern resembling a series of circular rose motifs surrounded by a twisted band edging. This border was used as carved decoration on furniture (plate 121).

Inlay

The removal of wood from a piece of furniture to a depth of about $\frac{1}{8}$in and its replacement with pieces of wood, bone or ivory of a contrasting colour to form a design or pattern. Mainly in use before c. 1660. Marquetry (qv) is sometimes loosely referred to as inlay but is rather different being a decorative veneer, and does not involve cutting into the carcase wood (plates 5, 101, 122).

Knee

The protruding top limb of a cabriole leg, frequently used on early eighteenth-century chairs for carved embellishment (plates 20, 22, 23, 26, 70, 72), or on early nineteenth-century furniture as a lobe at the top of a claw foot on a table (plates 96, 140).

Lacquer

A material made from the sap of a tree and used to varnish and produce a high lustre on decorated panels of wood. Lacquer panels were produced in China or Japan and exported in considerable quantities to Europe from the late seventeenth century onwards. Two main types exist: raised lacquer, in which the design is built up above the surface of the wood and gilded, the background usually being black or red; and incised or Coromandel lacquer, in which a layer of sand and fine clay is built up to a depth of about ½in, then lacquered, and has the design cut into it and coloured. The term lacquer is also applied loosely to European imitations of these materials, which are normally distinguished from true lacquer by the use of the term japan (plates 65, 68, 128).

Linenfold

A form of carved decoration, probably introduced from Flanders, popular in the early sixteenth century and said to resemble folds in linen. It was used to decorate panels in furniture or wall panelling (plate 3).

Lunette

A semi-circular motif with internal fan decoration used as a carved border on late sixteenth- and early seventeenth-century furniture (plate 59), and also found in marquetry or painted form on late eighteenth-century furniture.

Marquetry

The use of different types of wood, bone or ivory to construct a pattern or picture of a decorative nature in the form of a veneer. The term 'markatree' used in documents before *c.* 1660 refers to inlay (*qv*) (plates 105, 116, 133, 138, 178). See also *parquetry*.

Monopodia (singular: monopodium)

Legs or supports for tables, chairs and so on, shaped in the form of animal or human head and body, terminating in a single leg and foot. Particularly associated with early Regency design and the influence of Thomas Hope (plates 44, 87).

Necking

The reduction in thickness of the top of a leg or support, used particularly in chair legs of the Adam/Hepplewhite period (plate 35).

Neo-classicism

An international style which affected all forms of fine and decorative art from soon after the mid-eighteenth century for nearly a century, and was based upon a desire to seek perfection in classical form. The excavation of Herculaneum from 1738 onwards and of Pompeii ten years later, together with a new awareness of the influence and wealth of Greek art and architecture promoted the development of the style. In both architecture and interior decoration, including furniture, Robert Adam played an important part in the popularization of this style in Britain.

Ogee

An S-shaped moulding or outline (concave in the upper part and convex in the lower) (plate 123).

Ormolu

Gilt metal as in mounts used to decorate furniture, clocks, porcelain and so on. Before the 1760s ormolu mounts had to be imported, mainly from France, but from *c.* 1765 they were made in Birmingham by Mathew Boulton, while Diederick Nicholaus Anderson also produced ormolu until his death in 1769. The base metal was usually brass, which was coated with an amalgam of gold and mercury and then fired. The fumes given off when the mercury vaporized made the process very dangerous (plate 116).

Oyster-work

Parquetry (*qv*) involving the use of transversely cut veneers from a branch of 2in to 3in in diameter, which gives a repeated circular grain pattern. Veneers were made in this form from walnut, olive and laburnum and were used in the late seventeenth century on tables, chests of drawers and cabinets (plate 62).

Papier mâché

A hard and durable material made from pasting sheets of paper in moulds or pressing paper pulp between dies. Once dried the material was lacquered and painted. Inlay of mother of pearl was frequently incorporated. The industry was at the height of its popularity during the first half of Queen Victoria's reign, the firm of Jennens and Bettridge of Birmingham being one of the main producers. Chairs and small tables were commonly produced in this material, together with a wide range of boxes, trays and other small decorative articles (plate 54).

Parquetry

A veneer formed of woods selected for their colour or grain and usually arranged in geometrical patterns. In the late seventeenth century it was frequently used in the form of oyster-work (*qv*). It was also used to a limited extent in the late eighteenth and early nineteenth centuries, and a distinctive pattern of cubes in perspective was applied to decorative woodwork made in the Tunbridge Wells area in the nineteenth century (Tunbridge ware).

Patera
A round or oval decorative motif of classical origin much used on furniture of the late eighteenth century in the form of carving (plates 35, 82), marquetry (plates 81, 138) or painting.

Pediment
A shaped member extending above the line of the cornice in bookcases, cabinets, long-case clock cases and so on, especially on eighteenth-century furniture. Under the influence of architectural precedent the pediments, especially of the late Georgian period, are often broken in the centre to display some form of finial at this point. Some broken pediments are triangular while others are ogee-shaped and end in scrolls (swan neck pediments) (plates 129, 136).

Pie Crust Edge
A raised, carved edge frequently employed on tripod tables of the Chippendale period.

Pole lathe
A lathe operated by means of a treadle, for turning wood. A cord was passed round the object to be turned; it was fixed at one end to the treadle and at the other end to a pliant branch, which acted once the treadle was fully depressed to return the wood in the lathe to its starting position. This type of lathe was extensively used up to the beginning of the nineteenth century in the furniture trade and survived into the twentieth century in woodland areas where chair legs were produced on the spot, such as in the area round High Wycombe in Buckinghamshire.

Rail
A horizontal framing or constructional member (figures 1, 3).

Rake
A term used to describe the inclination of a chair back or leg from the perpendicular (plates 14, 15).

Reeding

The opposite of fluting. A moulding of parallel, raised, convex lines much used on Regency furniture for table and chair legs, friezes on tables and chests of drawers and so on (plate 43).

Rococo

A style of interior decoration which developed in France c. 1725 as a reaction against the heavy classical Baroque favoured at the court of Louis XIV. It appeared in Britain in the 1740s in the form of intricate shaping (C and S scrolls) and fanciful use of naturalistic forms. It is seen to its greatest advantage in carvers' work such as mirror frames (plates 164, 167). Furniture of the Chippendale period often reflects the Rococo taste (plates 28, 80).

Sabre legs

Chair legs of the Regency period; they are curved and resemble a sabre, imitating the form used on chairs illustrated in classical Greek vase painting (plates 42, 43, 46, 47).

Scagliola

A material made from marble chippings, alabaster and plaster in imitation of marble and as a cheaper substitute for it. This material also enabled intricate patterns, pictures and armorial bearings to be incorporated. Scagliola table tops were first used in the late seventeenth century but became more common in the eighteenth. At first they were imported from Italy but the art was being practised in Britain by the second half of the eighteenth century (plates 63, 64).

Secretaire

A writing desk with a sloping fall front with matching stand, popular c. 1700 (plate 143). The bureau, a similar type of desk but mounted on a case of drawers instead of a stand, developed at roughly the same period (plate 144). The term secretaire is also used for pieces of case furniture of the late eighteenth and nineteenth centuries where the top drawer lets down on a quadrant to act as a writing surface and exposes behind it drawers and compartments for writing materials. Often these are combined with a bookcase and are known as secretaire-bookcases (plate 137).

Shoulder board (or yoke)

The wide top-rail of Regency chairs which imitates the form of back adopted in the *klismos* illustrated on Greek vases (plates 43, 45, 47).

Spade foot

A tapering, rectangular block foot used on chairs, tables and other items of the Hepplewhite period (plates 39, 138, 151).

Splat

A vertical member in a chair back connecting the back seat rail to the top rail (plates 18, 19, 20, 22, 26).

Stretcher

A horizontal member joining the legs of a chair or table to give added strength (plates 11, 16, 17, 21).

Stile

A vertical framing member of a piece of furniture. See frame and panel construction (figures 1, 3).

Strapwork

Carved flat bands of decoration forming interconnected circles and other shapes, the space so enclosed sometimes being used for decorative motifs. This type of decoration is of Flemish and German origin and is very typical of late sixteenth- and early seventeenth-century furniture in England (plate 122).

Stringing

Narrow lines of a contrasting wood, metal, or other material (in the Regency period particularly of brass) incorporated in a veneer to provide either a border to a panel or for relief (plates 89, 91).

Swags

Festoons of fruit, leaves, flowers or other natural forms found in bold and heavy carving, especially on tables of the early eighteenth century (plates 66, 74). In the Adam period lighter swags of husks and bell flowers were often used for marquetry or painted decoration (plate 138).

Twist turning

A form of spiral turning frequently used on the legs of chairs and tables in the late seventeenth century (plate 61).

Vitruvian scroll

A classical border design consisting of a series of joined wave motifs and much used on furniture of the eighteenth century. It derives its name from the Roman architect Vitruvius, though it is known to have been in use at an earlier date (plates 73, 155).

Appendix 3
Chair leg designs
1600-1870

Types of baluster-turned chair legs—*second half 17th century*

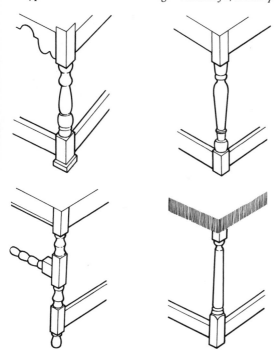

Chair legs—*early 17th century*

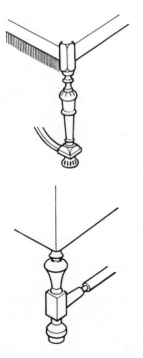
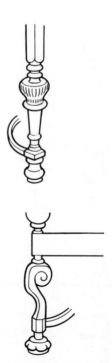

Forms of cabriole leg—*first half 18th century*

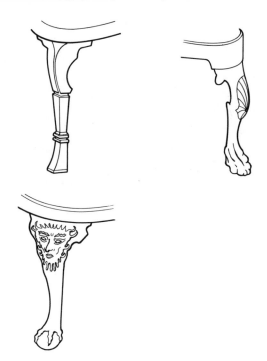

Chair legs—*late 18th century*

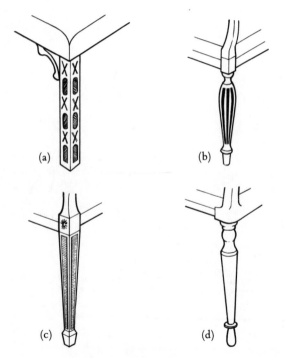

(a)

(b)

(c)

(d)

(a) "Chinese Chippendale"
(b), (c) and (d) Adam/Hepplewhite

Sheraton and Regency chair legs 1795–1830

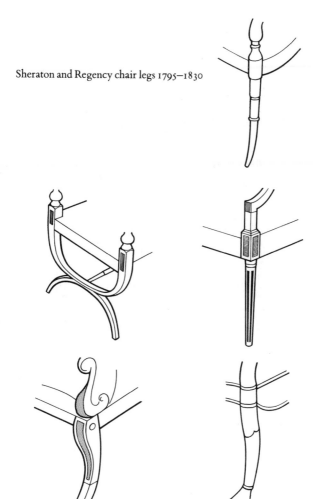

Victorian chair-legs 1830–70

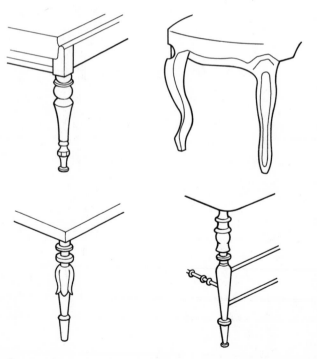

Appendix 4

Table of Furniture Periods

Date	Reign	Period in furniture history
1485 1509 1547 1553	Henry VII Henry VIII Edward VI Mary	EARLY TUDOR
1558	Elizabeth I	LATE TUDOR OR ELIZABETHAN
1603 1625	James I Charles I	JACOBEAN OR EARLY STUART
1649	The Commonwealth	COMMONWEALTH
1660 1685	Charles II James II	RESTORATION
1688	William III & Mary II	WILLIAM & MARY
1702	Anne	QUEEN ANNE
1714 1727	George I George II	EARLY GEORGIAN
1760	George III	CHIPPENDALE ADAM HEPPLEWHITE SHERATON REGENCY
1820	George IV	
1830	William IV	WILLIAM IV★
1837	Victoria	VICTORIAN
1901	Edward VII	

★The short reign of William IV did not establish any distinctive style of its own, but this term is used in the trade to denote pieces, probably Victorian in many cases, which although in the basic Grecian tradition of the Regency show shaping of heaviness of detail associated with Victorian taste.

Important designers and craftsmen	*Main periods of architecture and interior design in Britain*
	ENGLISH RENAISSANCE
Daniel Marot Jean Pelletier Gerreit Jensen	ENGLISH BAROQUE
William Kent Thomas Chippendale..................... Thomas Johnson John Linnell John Mayhew & William Ince Robert Adam George Hepplewhite Thomas Shearer Thomas Sheraton Thomas Hope George Smith	PALLADIAN NEO-CLASSICAL GREEK REVIVAL ARCHITECTURE OF THE PICTURESQUE
A. W. N. Pugin William Burgess William Morris L. W. Godwin	ITALIANATE GOTHIC REVIVAL

Index